YOUNG PROFESSIONALS

Ian Stannard

Young Professionals

This first edition published in 2010 by Trotman Publishing, an imprint of Crimson Publishing, Westminster House, Kew Road, Richmond, Surrey TW9 2ND.

© Trotman Publishing 2010
Author: Ian Stannard
ISBN: 978-1-84455-2-351
British Library Cataloguing in Publications data
A catalogue record for this book is available from the British Library

Typeset by: RefineCatch Ltd
Printed and bound by: TJ International Ltd, Padstow, Cornwall

YOUNG PROFESSIONALS

CONTENTS

ABOUT THE AUTHOR

Ian Stannard is the Head of Careers and Higher Education at Christ's Hospital School in Sussex, an independent mixed boarding school which sends 95% of its pupils into higher education every year. Ian is responsible for the school's UCAS, CUKAS, Oxbridge and overseas applications.

Ian is the author of *How to Write a Winning UCAS Personal Statement*, also published by Trotman.

ACKNOWLEDGMENTS

Writing a book is not an easy task and it requires a great deal of support and assistance. This book is no different; in fact, the assistance required has been greater than most. I am therefore grateful to all those who have helped me in any way.

I would like to name a few people and companies in particular who deserve special mention. The first is Alison Yates, who commissioned the book in the first instance; and Jessica Spencer, who has been so helpful in the final stages. Their advice and expertise has been invaluable. I am also most grateful to the companies, organisations and universities that have provided me with information and advice. These include GCHQ, MI5, MI6, Drivers Jonas Deloitte, Arup, Lloyds Banking Group, Channel 4, Freshfields Law, the Royal Veterinary College, RICS, JP Morgan Brighton and Sussex Medical School, Engineering UK, Swansea University, Essex University, City University London, and representatives from the Civil Service, armed forces and police service.

Without their assistance, this book would not be able to claim to represent the current mood of the professions in the UK and their desire to recruit from the widest possible base. I am most grateful for their help.

Thanks too, of course, to my wife Jenny and children Harry and Emily for their support and patience.

CHAPTER 1

WHAT IS A PROFESSION?

Why is this book for me?

This book provides an accurate and interesting insight into all the major professions in the UK today. All the information has been drawn from the latest sources and in many cases it comes direct from the professional bodies or companies themselves.

It is written for you, the student, particularly pupils at Key Stage 4. This is because at this stage in your education you have to make important decisions that may affect your ability to get into the profession of your choice. The most important of these will be what to study after your GCSEs.

Too many bright pupils in schools up and down the country think that they are not capable of becoming a lawyer, dentist, engineer, civil servant or investment banker. This may be because they come from a family that has never sent someone to university or simply because they lack confidence in their ability. Aspiration and self-esteem is a crucial factor too – they need people in school and at home to push them on to succeed.

It might also be due to the fact that they think the professions are stuffy, not interested in people like them or only looking for graduates from Oxford or Cambridge. This is simply not true: every profession in the UK is now looking to recruit clever pupils just like you, the reader of this book!

This book is written for bright pupils who aspire to join the professions, mostly via university. As a result it does target those that are academically able. They do not need to be AAA students but should have the potential to gain entry into higher education and then a profession in a competitive market where high academic standards normally apply.

This in turn will please the government, which is promoting fair access to all professions and which wants to increase social mobility (a person's ability to move from one social class to another) in the UK. The main reason for this is that it wants all students to feel that they can achieve their ambitions regardless of their background. In other words, you do not have to come from a rich family to succeed. You need to work hard at school: but if you do that, any profession is open to you.

All the professions in the UK are fully signed up to this ethos and are looking to recruit people from all backgrounds. They want to hear from you, so aim high!

So what is a profession?

There is no one single definition of what a profession is. However, on the whole the following are true.

- Most professions have standard qualification requirements. This means that you either take a qualification at university (for instance, a doctor takes a degree in medicine) or you take professional qualifications once you start work.
- Most professions have governing bodies that set out clear rules of conduct that both companies and individuals must follow. For instance, the Law Society regulates solicitors.
- Many professional people consider that their work is vocational. The word 'vocation' comes from the Latin word for 'calling'. It is a job that a person feels especially drawn towards, one that they are suited to and for which they have trained and qualified. Good examples are teaching and the medical professions.
- Most professions expect their employees to work to high standards and encourage people to carry on training throughout their career. This is called continuing professional development (CPD). Learning does not stop at school or college – it is life long!

UK PROFESSIONS ARE WORLD LEADERS!

- Our armed forces are respected worldwide as highly trained professionals.
- The City of London is home to many of the world's banks, law firms, insurance brokers and consultancy firms. Even after the recent collapse in the world financial markets and the resulting recession, these institutions still generate billions of pounds in profits and employ tens of thousands of people worldwide.

■ Britain is a global leader in healthcare. Our pharmaceutical industry spends £3.3 billion on research and development every year.

■ We train cutting-edge architects who work around the globe, designing buildings on every continent.

■ Our journalists, TV companies and advertising agencies are world renowned, as indeed are our hospitals, schools, police service and Civil Service.

What are the professions?

Again, this is a difficult question to answer. There are over 130 professional sectors in the UK and they employ 11 million people. These include:

■ health service professionals, such as vets, doctors, dentists, nurses, physiotherapists and child psychologists

■ legal professionals, such as solicitors, barristers, paralegals and court officials

■ management and business service professionals, such as accountants, bankers, management consultants and financial advisers

■ creative industry professionals, such as journalists, publishers, designers, public relations (PR) consultants and artists

■ public service professionals, such as senior civil servants, managers in local government, senior police officers and armed forces officers

■ scientists, such as chemists, pharmacologists and mathematicians

■ education professionals throughout the age range, from infant school teachers to university professors

■ building and engineering professionals, such as architects, surveyors, engineers and town planners.

This book includes detailed profiles of many of the professions mentioned above, including information about what it is like to work in that profession, the key skills employers look for in an applicant, what educational qualifications you need, the long-term salary and job prospects and where to find out more. Each profile contains up-to-date facts and will, we hope, debunk some of the myths surrounding the profession – and with them your own uncertainty about whether you are the 'right sort of person' to join that profession in the future.

The demand for professionals in the UK is growing. At the moment 2.25 million people work in local government, 1.4 million in the NHS, 500,000 in engineering, 200,000 in the law and 700,000 in teaching. These numbers are likely to increase, along with other professions, in the next decade. The largest growth will be in the creative and fashion industry, with thousands more places for people designing clothes, computer games and online content.

EMPLOYMENT IN THE UK IS CHANGING FAST!

In 1900 very few jobs in the UK were professional. By 1951, one in every eight jobs in the UK was a professional post. By 2001, the figure was one in three, and by 2025 this figure is projected to rise to one in two.

The reasons for this are varied, but essentially it is down to a few key factors.

- More women now work than ever before. This trend started in the Second World War and now women have careers in every profession.
- Manufacturing in the UK has declined steadily, with factory employment opportunities being replaced by new jobs in retail, the service sector and the new professions.
- More people are going to university than ever before. More of these graduates are joining the professions.

The changing face of the professions

All the major professional bodies are committed to raising the number of applications they receive from groups in society who are currently under-represented in the professions.

Who are these people?

- Men and women who have not grown up in families with parents who are professionals.
- Men and women whose families earn less than the national average income (£25,000).
- Men and women who have studied as mature students (i.e. they went to university after the age of 23).
- Men and women who are from ethnic minorities.
- Men and women who have a disability.

As I mentioned earlier, the key message is that the professions are open to all, regardless of age, gender, race, religious belief or class. The professions actively seek applications from the groups listed above, and I hope that this book will also go some way to increase the number of applications from people in these groups.

Starting early

You probably already know that it is very important to work hard at school to achieve the best grades you can. All your hard effort now will pay off in the future. Choosing your GCSE and AS/A2 subjects is also very important. If you feel unsure, do seek help from a careers teacher or look at one of the many websites that can help you. One very good site is www.connexions-direct. com. This is a very comprehensive site with loads of relevant and up-to-date information about courses, careers and your options at the ages of 14, 16 and 18.

As you are reading this, I assume that you want to do well at school and go to university too. You might be the first person in your family to think about this. If so, great! You might find the Aimhigher website useful – it contains plenty of advice about higher and further education. Google 'Aim Higher' to find your local Aimhigher website.

Higher education and widening participation

Since 1997, millions of pounds has been invested in widening access to university; the aim was to increase social mobility by achieving a target (now dropped) of 50% of all school leavers entering university. While all the universities have signed up to this agenda and employ staff to promote it, sadly it is still the case that for many people from homes that are not considered middle class, university remains a pipe dream.

While more people than ever are going to university, the universities are still very keen to attract people from particular groups in society. It is clear that too few people from disadvantaged backgrounds apply. Universities have introduced many initiatives to encourage young people from these areas to apply: some run free taster courses or other activities with the aim of raising aspirations and achievement, for example by providing advice and guidance at increasingly younger ages, and offering role models through mentoring.

If you are keen to go to university, but feel out of your depth, contact the university nearest home and ask about their widening participation projects. They will be delighted to hear from you – they will be supportive and encouraging and keen to answer your questions. Indeed, they will do all they can to make you feel happy and wanted. They want you to ring or email them. That is the first step to realising **your** dream – so stop thinking about it and start living it!

CHAPTER 2

WHAT NEXT AFTER SCHOOL?

Let's assume for a moment that you are doing well at school. You already have or are on course for a decent set of GCSEs and are now doing or contemplating A levels (or equivalent). You may be thinking – what next after school?

If you are considering university I very strongly recommend that you **go for it**. It will change your life for the better and open doors for you that would otherwise be closed. Don't worry if you are the first in your class or your family to think about this. Be proud of your achievements and remember that the best companies in the world are looking to employ people just like you. Yes – you!

So why go to university?

The simple answer is that most of the top professions in the UK look for graduates to fill the jobs on offer. Some professions demand that you have a degree in a particular subject. However, the desire to be a professional is not the only reason to aim high and win a place at university.

Employment prospects

With more than a third of those leaving school at 18 going on to university (compared with 10% 25 years ago), the competition for 'graduate' jobs has increased. This leads to the assumption that many graduates will be working in what were hitherto jobs for people who left school after A levels. This in turn will mean the financial advantage of having a degree will be eroded as the number of graduates increases in these types of jobs.

Taking this scenario further, non-graduates will be pushed further down the queue for the best jobs. On this basis you've nothing to lose by applying. Aim high and remember that universities want people from all walks of life to apply. Indeed, if you are from an under-represented group they will often offer you special help to achieve your ambition.

Prior to the present economic downturn, graduate starting salaries were in the order of £21,000 (£25,000 in London). However, the number of vacancies in most areas of employment has been severely reduced and data is not yet available for starting salaries in 2010. The positive point being that by the time you graduate, the economy should have recovered!

It is likely that the rate of salary increases in London and elsewhere will not be as rapid as in past years, and promoting the more successful graduates will be viewed as a way of avoiding the kind of regular salary increases that were common in the past.

Employment prospects in the immediate future are not expected to be rosy, but it is probable that graduates will be better placed to benefit in the job market than those without a degree.

Self-development

Higher education is not just about obtaining a degree. It is an opportunity to develop into a more rounded individual; and one who will be more attractive to employers.

Personal development is a major by-product of going to university. Studying at university will develop your confidence as you'll meet a wide range of students both from the UK and from overseas. This interaction will broaden your views and enable you to be a more critical thinker through hearing other people's experiences and viewpoints. This skill will be useful both socially and during your tutorials and later in your working life.

Having to fend for yourself is an important part of self-development. The independence gained from this experience will be of great benefit when dealing with people in a work environment. The need to plan, organise, communicate, participate in teams, work independently – and a host of other transferable skills – are invaluable.

Developing greater confidence and self-esteem helps you perform better at interview, makes you more willing to take on new tasks and apply for promotion, and can result in higher salaries through improved performance. The skills already mentioned can also help you manage people and are useful in all walks of life. Without those personal skills, it is unlikely that you will be able to undertake managerial roles.

The value of higher education

Going to university is not just about obtaining a degree; it is about the whole life experience. The equation is: obtaining a degree will cost you money, resulting in debts; but set against this is the long-term benefit in terms of employment opportunities.

Remember, the student loan is an interest-free loan and you do not start repaying it until you are earning the equivalent of £15,000 per annum. The repayment is made at the rate of 9% of any income above this level. The extra income a graduate will earn more than covers the loan repayment, so in purely monetary terms the qualification is worthwhile.

Do not be scared off by debt – most students live with debt and manage it well. Many universities also have very good bursary and hardship funds designed to help people, perhaps like you, who come from a family who cannot help them out financially. The money is out there if you need it. If in doubt, talk to the welfare office of a university near you. This short-term debt is **well worth** the long-term benefits.

As the graduate workforce increases, competition for jobs will increase, but this will add more pressure to those leaving school after A levels to get jobs with good prospects.

Life skills developed at university – such as confidence, independence or ability to mix with a diverse range of people – will stand you in good stead in the workplace. Student surveys indicate that students believe money spent on education is a good investment for their future.

CHAPTER 3

WHAT KIND OF PROFESSIONAL COULD I BE?

This is a question that many young people ask when they begin to think about GCSEs and A levels. This is the advice I would give, based on years of answering similar questions.

What GCSEs should I do?

The simple answer is that you will need to have a good set of GCSE or IGCSE results to gain access to university and hence the professions. This is because a good set of GCSE grades allows you to study A levels or something similar such as the International Baccalaureate (IB). These grades, together with the GCSE results you achieve(d) at 16 years of age, go a long way towards securing you a place on the course of your dreams at university.

Some GCSE subjects are compulsory in all schools. These are English, maths and science. (Some schools offer combined science and others single sciences.) In addition, you are encouraged to take a modern foreign language, an arts subject such as art, music, drama or media studies, and at least one humanities subject, for example history, religious studies, geography or sociology.

My general advice is not to worry too much – do what you enjoy and what you are good at. Don't do what your friends are doing unless you also enjoy the subject. After all, it is you who will be taking the exam in the end. Don't choose a subject because you like the teacher – sometimes they leave!

The vast majority of universities, including Oxford and Cambridge, just want to see good grades. To enter top universities in the UK you should aim for A* to B grades in all your subjects. The odd C is not a disaster – but it should be a rarity.

What A levels should I take?

Throughout this book I will refer to AS or A2 levels. Clearly this is not the only option on offer, but it is the most popular. If you decide to stay in full-time education after Year 11, there are a range of academic, work-related and skills-based qualifications you can potentially use to get into higher education.

Generally, you'll need qualifications at Level 3 on the National Qualifications Framework. For UK students, this usually means:

- A levels
- International Baccalaureate (IB)
- Pre-U
- Scottish Highers
- Advanced Diploma
- National Vocational Qualifications (NVQs)
- Scottish Vocational Qualifications (SVQs)
- BTEC National Certificates and Diplomas

I will focus on A levels (or equivalent), but the advice in this book is useful whichever route you choose to follow.

To get the most out of studying after the age of 16 (sometimes known as further education or FE), it's important to take time to choose the right courses and qualifications.

Key dos and don'ts

Do:

- choose those subjects that you are good at and enjoy – that way there is a better than average chance you will get the grades you need
- choose subjects that you have studied before. You can't always follow this advice because some A levels (such as media studies, philosophy and history of art) are not offered at GCSE. However, as a general rule of thumb you are advised to not study an A level if you are unlikely to get a minimum of a grade B at GCSE. An A at GCSE is really the minimum you need to have a realistic chance of getting an A or B at A2

- if you have a good idea what profession you want to get into, check to see if they require any specific type of degree. For instance, engineers study engineering, architects study architecture and doctors study medicine. Entry requirements for each of these will expect you to have studied one or more specific subjects at A level. The way to be sure is to check online. You could look at www.ucas.com, which has all the courses open to you and information about what A levels and skills universities are looking for. Alternatively, go to your local university's website and see what they are looking for. The key is proper, careful research

- remember that all your results matter and the AS results you put on your UCAS form (the form you fill in when applying to university) will include all your grades. So work hard in Year 12!

Don't:

- do what your friends are doing. This is a recipe for disaster
- do a subject because you like a teacher – teachers leave!
- do subjects that you do not enjoy simply because you think you want to be a 'doctor' or 'engineer'. For instance, if you do not like chemistry you will probably not do well and therefore you will not get into medicine anyway. Play to your strengths
- listen too hard to your parents. They want the best for you, but some parents can influence their children in a way that is unhelpful, pushing them into a course that they want them to do but is not really ideal for their son or daughter
- think that you are not 'good' enough or not the right sort of person to get into a top university. This is negative thinking and plain rubbish. If you are bright enough, the options open to you are as wide as anyone else's. Aim high – do not let other people's pessimism or cynical comments put you off.

Two good books that you might find helpful are *Choosing Your A-Levels and Other Post-16 Options* by Gary Woodward and *Which A Levels? The Guide to Choosing Your AS and A Levels* by the experienced education author Alison Dixon.

What profession should I aim for?

This is a question that is almost impossible to answer without meeting you. However, these general rules of thumb are worth considering.

■ Aim high. No matter what your background, if you have the talent you should take the opportunity to fulfil your potential. The government and professional bodies that support the professions in the UK are all committed to widening the field of applicants to all professions. They want to break down stereotypes, open up opportunities for all and increase social mobility as a result. The message is simple: if you have the ambition, go for it.

■ What are your strengths? These include both your academic and your personal strengths. Take time to write down the subjects that you excel in and feel passionate about. Then write down an honest list of your personal strengths and weaknesses. Are you a team player? Are you a leader? Do you enjoy a challenge? Would you like to work in an environment that rewards creativity? Do you want to work in an organisation that rewards hard work but in turn expects its employees to work hard for those rewards?

Some professions demand specific academic skills – others do not. I refer to A levels here for ease, but if you are taking an alternative route such as the Diploma route, IB or Pre-U, the same applies with slight modifications. In every case, check the UCAS database (www.ucas.com) to see what each course demands.

The list below gives some general information about what qualifications are needed to enter each of the broad professional categories.

■ The **armed forces and security services** don't in general have specific academic demands, but the Army, Royal Air Force (RAF) and Navy all look to recruit engineers and the Secret Service and GCHQ (Government Communications Headquarters) look for expert linguists, IT specialists and electrical engineers.

■ **Banks and other financial organisations** are open to all applicants, but in some cases mathematics, physics and economics would be an advantage.

■ The **building and construction industry** looks for professional and degree qualifications in, for example, surveying. These in turn demand certain subjects that you may be obliged to take at A level. Companies recruiting **architects** expect appropriate qualifications that can only be achieved with certain A levels. Many architecture courses look for evidence of a portfolio of work, which may mean that A level Art is a route to success.

- The **Civil Service** has no particular academic demands other than a good degree and evidence of leadership potential and personal ambition.
- **Engineering** companies expect you to have an engineering degree. Most of these courses specify mathematics, physics and sometimes chemistry at A level.
- **Law** does not look for any particular degree but does require professional qualifications that can be taken in one year if you hold a law degree and in two years if you don't.
- **Marketing, advertising and PR** companies are happy to accept applicants from all degree disciplines but will look favourably on a candidate with either creative or marketing qualifications.
- The **media** sector is open to all, regardless of degree subject.
- **Medicine** and careers allied to medicine will expect high grades in chemistry and biology. You will also need to show that you appreciate the demands of the profession by undertaking sufficient work experience.
- The **teaching** profession expects all applicants to have achieved Qualified Teacher Status (QTS). This can be done through a number of routes, including studying for an undergraduate education degree with QTS status or studying for an undergraduate degree in any subject and then taking a PGCE (Postgraduate or Professional Graduate Certificate in Education). With the right accreditation you can teach students in early years education through to those studying at higher education institutions.
- **Vets** need to take sciences at A level to be admitted to a course leading to a veterinary qualification.

CHAPTER 4

ARCHITECTURE AND SURVEYING

An introduction to architecture and surveying

An architect is given a brief to design a structure to meet the needs of a client. This might be an individual wanting an extension on a house or a multinational company looking to build a new headquarters. Other projects might include sports stadiums, tunnels, bridges, airports, hotels or hospitals. The range of opportunities to test your skills is huge and the rewards in terms of pay and prestige for top architects can be significant.

Surveying is a wide-ranging profession covering a diverse mix of areas, including construction projects, land surveying, mineral extraction, marine projects and town planning. Surveyors work closely with architects, engineers and builders in the initial design phase of projects, making sure that plans meet strict legal and health and safety guidelines.

Architect

What do architects do?

An architect is a skilled professional who works in the building and construction industry. Most are graduates and they are normally artistic, creative and scientific. They need to have a vision of how something would look while at the same time understanding enough about physics to ensure that it will not fall down!

Some architects are self-employed and others work for large companies or government bodies. They work closely with engineers, designers, surveyors, lawyers and sometimes town planners and landscape gardeners. They may be asked to design new buildings from scratch, or to extend existing buildings, restore an old building or change the use of a building – a good example being the conversion of an old barn on a farm into flats. Some architects work with governments or companies to build landmark buildings or structures that become internationally famous, such as Wembley Stadium, the Millennium Dome or the Channel Tunnel. Others only work for individuals, perhaps designing an extension for a family home or converting a roof space into a new bedroom.

Key skills required

- Good spatial awareness and a creative mind; a keen interest in how people react to different kinds of building and the environment that surrounds them. Many architects have studied art or design technology at school.

- An awareness of current trends and fashions in building and landscape design, with an eye to ways in which a design can reduce energy costs post-construction.

- Environmental awareness.

- Architects need to be organised and efficient in their planning and preparation. Final designs must be meticulous to conform to strict building regulations and avert problems later in the building phase.

- Good IT skills are very important. Most architectural designs are now produced using computer-aided design (CAD) software. In addition, an architect should have a sound grasp of physics and mathematics.

- Good interpersonal skills are vital, as the needs of the clients are paramount when preparing and presenting design proposals to clients, often in a competitive environment.

- An architect must be happy to work in a group as well as on their own. They will also need to be able to communicate well with a diverse range of professionals and tradespeople. On every project, architects work closely with other professionals, including engineers, surveyors, architectural technicians and technologists, to make sure that their buildings meet the necessary standards. Meeting the needs and concerns of local residents is increasingly important too.

- They will be required to visit sites regularly to co-ordinate the work of contractors, anticipate potential problems and solve them swiftly. Most architects are called upon to work in sometimes stressful situations and to meet tight deadlines. They often oversee a project from beginning to end.

Entry routes

To practise as an architect, and use the title architect, individuals must register with the Architects Registration Board (ARB). This means spending at least seven years in training and higher education, which consists of:

- five years of study on a recognised course consisting of the three-year Royal Institute of British Architects (RIBA)/ARB Part 1 and the two-year RIBA/ARB Part 2
- at least two years' training in an architect's office
- passing an RIBA/ARB Part 3 Examination in Professional Practice and Management.

There are over 40 institutions validated by RIBA and prescribed by the ARB to offer Parts 1, 2 and 3.

When conducting my research I looked at a number of different universities that offer such courses. Most follow a similar pattern and expect similar skills from potential applicants. They expect high academic standards; many top schools now expect you to have at least AAB at A2. Few expect any particular mix of A levels, but an increasing number look favourably on A level Art. This is principally because the skills you learn as an artist, combined with an awareness of physics, help develop the spatial awareness and drawing skills that most architecture courses demand. Most schools will ask to see a portfolio of freehand drawings and sketches: these are not sent at the time of application but are assessed at interview. Some universities also offer a Foundation course for those students without the usual mix of qualifications. This is a one-year preparatory course taken prior to starting the degree proper.

Training and development

Training has to include at least two years working in an architect's office. Normally, one year is spent after Part 1 and the second year after Part 2 of the RIBA/ARB examinations. The trainee then has to pass the RIBA/ARB Part 3 Examination in Professional Practice and Management to be able to register as an architect. Part 3 includes demonstrating a minimum of 2 years professional experience, and a written and oral examination.

Once qualified, architects are required to keep up to date by undertaking mandatory continuing professional development (CPD), which might include a combination of short courses, higher-level qualifications, staff development and training.

Job prospects

As with all building and construction jobs, the work tends to be plentiful in times of economic growth and declines during more austere economic circumstances. The vast majority of the 30,000 architects in the UK work in private practice or in small- to medium-sized firms that specialise in particular types of project. Competition is fierce, so your success will depend on your ability to anticipate trends, meet clients' needs and produce designs that are efficient in terms of cost and carbon footprint.

Many architects work for central and local government, construction companies and commercial and industrial organisations such as retailers and manufacturers.

Most jobs for architects are in London and southeast England, where most of the larger practices are based, but it is possible to work in smaller practices anywhere in the UK.

The professional bodies for architecture include job vacancies on their websites. There are also vacancies in the professional magazines and journals such as *Architects' Journal*, published jointly with Careers in Construction, the UK's largest specialist construction recruitment website.

Salary

Newly qualified architects (with RIBA Part 3) can earn approximately £28,000 a year. A more established architect might expect to earn up to £40,000, unless they become a partner in a larger firm, where the salaries can be much higher.

Further information

- Royal Institute of British Architects (RIBA), 66 Portland Place, London W1B 1AD. Tel: 020 7580 5533
- www.architecture.com
- www.riba-jobs.com

Chartered surveyor

What do chartered surveyors do?

Surveying is a generic term that covers a variety of roles in the built environment, from residential to commercial. They include agency work, construction project management, town planning and valuation. Surveyors essentially measure, value, protect and enhance the world's physical assets and they're involved in a vast array of projects. Think of all the physical assets on the earth – buildings, trees, airports, antiques, festivals, hotels, rainforests, ports and harbours: surveyors are involved in all of these and play an important role in shaping the world we live in.

Surveying practices range in size from just three members of staff up to international multidisciplinary firms employing thousands of people. Anyone from any background can make a career in chartered surveying: if you have the desire, there are plenty of opportunities. Age is also not an issue. The quicker you can get into a graduate scheme, the sooner you can get chartered. To be chartered you need to be admitted to the Royal Institute of Chartered Surveyors. This requires that you have taken examinations and professional courses that mean you can operate at the very highest level of this profession. Membership implies you are a very able and highly-qualified surveyor. Surveying is a diverse and exciting career choice that can give you the opportunity to travel the world and meet all kinds of people.

Historically, projects would be managed by architects; nowadays project managers manage everything. They're in the thick of things, taking responsibility, experiencing the excitement and reaping the glory of a project, for example an Olympic stadium, a football ground, Crossrail.

A client will come to the project managers with a concept. The project managers will work closely with the client through the processes of finding the money/investment, finding a site, planning, the architect's involvement and all the steps until the project is finally built.

Chartered surveying is not a single career, but a group of careers with certain skills in common, and as a result chartered surveyors work in many different fields. Some of these are listed below.

■ **Arts and antiques:** through the ages, artists and craftsmen have created fabulous objects that reveal the history and fashion of every continent. Chartered arts and antiques surveyors are privileged to work with valuable and curious artefacts, advising the owners on their value, care, sale and acquisition – privately or by auction.

- **Commercial property:** surveyors in this sector are involved in the purchase, sale, management and leasing of business premises, negotiations between landlords and tenants, and strategic management of corporate property portfolios, as well as developing infrastructure for telecoms networks and valuing land and buildings.
- **Dispute resolution:** rent reviews, lease renewals, building contracts, boundary disputes, valuation, planning disputes and professional negligence, as well as advising on conflict avoidance and acting as arbitrators, adjudicators, mediators and experts.
- **Facilities management:** the total management of the services that support a business including relocation, health and safety, outsourcing, procurement, property management and utilities and services.
- **Machinery and business assets:** valuation and sale of a firm's machinery, equipment and business assets (from oil refineries to websites), which are important for insurance, accounting, insolvency, compulsory purchase, taxation and market value purposes.
- **Management consultancy:** involves providing impartial advice. A management consultant could be involved with developing a real-estate acquisition plan, a local authority leisure strategy or a corporate recovery programme, handling insolvency or helping a manufacturer overcome production problems.
- **Residential property:** the specialism with the highest public profile. It can involve acting as an agent, broker or auctioneer in a sale, the management, valuation and surveying of public or private property, and overseeing the contractual relationship between landlords and tenants, as well as giving advice on investment and development.
- **Valuation:** valuation of property, land and business assets is a core skill that plays a vital role in bank lending, accounting, investment, taxation and many other activities.

Key skills required

- A basic grasp of maths.
- Good written and spoken English.
- IT literacy.
- Creativity; an interest in design.

- A practical approach to problem solving.
- Excellent negotiating skills.
- A methodical approach; attention to detail.
- Ability to work well with people at all levels.
- A logical mind.
- Good people and project management skills.
- Ability to co-ordinate a number of different projects at the same time.

Entry routes

If you want to be the best surveyor possible, you need to be chartered. In the chartered surveyors' case this is done by the Royal Institution of Chartered Surveyors (RICS).

In return for the hard work and dedication you put in to becoming fully qualified and achieving chartered status, you will earn the right to use the letters MRICS (Member of the RICS) after your name. Employers and clients around the world recognise this as a mark of quality in the surveying professions, and because of this global recognition, chartered status is the gateway to numerous job and career opportunities.

For a RICS-accredited degree course, the qualifications needed are generally three A levels or a relevant BTEC national award, plus at least five GCSEs (A*–C) or equivalent. Useful A level subjects include English, geography, maths, the physical sciences, geology, economics, law, IT, art, business studies, languages, and design and technology. The Diploma in Construction and the Built Environment and the Diploma in Environmental and Land-based Studies may also be relevant. Entry requirements vary, so check with individual institutions.

Applicants can also take a first degree not accredited by RICS followed by an accredited postgraduate conversion course. Useful first degree subjects include geography, mathematics, economics and physical sciences.

Large companies in this area, such as Drivers Jonas Deloitte, take on graduates and train them to become chartered: they have to complete an Assessment of Professional Competence (APC). The APC process is designed to ensure that you are established as a competent member of the profession once you graduate and join the world of work. This involves a period of structured training,

ROYAL INSTITUTION OF CHARTERED SURVEYORS

What is RICS?

RICS – The Royal Institution of Chartered Surveyors – is the world's leading qualification when it comes to professional standards in land, property and construction. Over 100,000 property professionals working in the major established and emerging economies of the world have already recognised the importance of securing RICS status by becoming members.

RICS is an independent professional body originally established in the UK by Royal Charter. Since 1868, RICS has been committed to setting and upholding the highest standards of excellence and integrity – providing impartial, authoritative advice on key issues affecting businesses and society. RICS is a regulator of both its individual members and firms enabling it to maintain the highest standards and providing the basis for unparalleled client confidence in the sector.

CHARTERED SURVEYOR PROFILES

Emily Speak MRICS, Valuation surveyor, King Sturge, Manchester

Television production may seem a world away from surveying, but Emily Speak's experience of the former eventually led her into a career in the latter.

On completion of her performing arts degree aged 21, Emily headed to London where she worked as a freelance location manager for television and film. But it wasn't quite as glamorous or as exciting as you'd expect.

"After around five years I became frustrated with the lack of balance between work and life, so I sought an alternative career that would provide more normal working hours, stability, variety and an opportunity to meet new people," says Emily.

She thought that surveying might be what she'd been looking for, and after doing work experience in Manchester at King Sturge and DTZ, Emily undertook a masters degree in commercial property management at Liverpool John Moores University. She then joined King Sturge as a graduate where she worked in the management team. In the short time she's been there, Emily has even spent six months in France working with her company's Paris valuation team.

Back in Manchester, her current position as valuation surveyor requires Emily to work on portfolio valuations, as well as industrial, office and retail valuations for loan security or re-finance. She was keen to become a member of the RICS, to benefit from being part of a professional entity, so she took her Assessment of Professional Competence (APC), and has recently passed.

When I started training for my APC, I wrote a work diary on a weekly basis, and kept up-to-date by reading Estates Gazette and Property Week. I also attended regular in-house training sessions and external seminars with a view to developing my experience and knowledge," she explains.

While Emily found it quite challenging to obtain a holistic background of knowledge and experience, the regular training and guidance from her peers helped her through it.

My advice to anyone embarking on the APC would be that it's not easy, but if you prepare then it will pay off. Cramming at the last minute will only cheat yourself as you will find that if you do qualify you won't understand things!"

Asmau Nasir-Lawal MRICS, John Rowan & Partners LLP, London Senior project manager

Asmau is the perfect example of someone who has successfully worked her way up the career ladder. Starting out as a student surveyor in a general practice firm, she is now the Senior project manager of John Rowan & Partners LLP. One of the most respected projects that she has worked on was 17 St Augustine's Road, London. The project aimed at reducing the CO2 emissions in this Victorian building by 90% and won three industry awards, including the Inside Housing's 2008 Sustainability Housing Awards as the winner of the Low Energy Upgraded Social Housing Project of the Year.

After studying for a BSc in Estate Management at Obafemi Awolowo University, Ile-Ife in Nigeria before moving to the UK, she took a MSc in Project Management at the University of Greenwich, London. She describes surveying as "a multi-dimensional career where every day brings a new challenge" and it was her keen interest in the structure of buildings that spurred her into becoming a surveyor.

Every day is varied and this was certainly true when she was called to survey a bathroom, which was located on the lower ground floor of a three-storey back addition. "The resident had noticed the ceiling bowing slightly while decorating," Asmau explains. "It turns out the ceiling was a York stone slab and was the only thing supporting the two upper floors. You never know what a day at work will bring."

Asmau decided to take the APC as she felt it was the next logical step in her career. A lot of time and dedication was required but she feels it was worth it, "It means a lot to become a part of an internationally recognised institution and be acknowledged as a professional not only by colleagues but by clients and the wider public."

The advice that Asmau gives to people who want to embark on taking the APC is to work hard, make sacrifices and learn a lot. "Extra work was required and one had to be able to combine and prioritise everything in order to balance work, studying for the APC and home/social life". But she believes that becoming chartered has been the highlight of her career.

Surveying is Asmau's dream job and she aspires to work on bigger projects, gain more experience and keep learning, "There are always new things to do and other projects to get involved with."

keeping a log book of relevant work experience, and a final assessment, where a group of trained assessors will ask you questions to decide whether you are professionally competent.

The RICS qualification is recognised as the mark of property professionalism worldwide and as such it is widely seen as the 'gold standard' in postgraduate professional surveying qualifications.

Job prospects

Surveyors are employed throughout the UK, but there are more jobs in large cities, particularly London. There is considerable competition for graduate jobs with leading surveying firms.

In the private sector, employers include surveying practices, property companies, consultancies, construction companies, estate agencies, housing associations and large organisations that own land (such as retailers, utility companies and financial institutions). In the public sector, employers include local authorities, government departments, hospital trusts and universities.

CASE STUDY: MARK UNDERWOOD
BA(HONS) MPHIL AIEMA MRTPI, DIRECTOR

Mark has worked at Drivers Jonas Deloitte since 1997. He began his career in the firm's London office and moved to work from Manchester in 2000. He spent 2007/08 heading up and establishing the Drivers Jonas Deloitte Leeds planning team and returned to London in June 2008. He now works in Drivers Jonas Deloitte's city office in the Development Consulting group.

He has broad experience in the planning system, including the submission of planning applications, expert witness advice in connection with planning and related inquiries, and planning advice of a general nature. Mark is also accredited by the Institute of Environmental Management and Assessment and is a specialist in preparing and managing major planning applications and Environmental Impact Assessments. He is currently involved in a range of constructions throughout the UK: hospitals; educational, retail, leisure and residential facilities; business parks; and industrial schemes.

Winner of the Northwest Young Property Professional of the Year 2007, his achievements include expanding the Drivers Jonas Deloitte Planning team in Manchester, working with Manchester City Council on securing the location of the UK's first super casino, advising Ballymore on an application for a 60-storey tower at Manchester Piccadilly, and working with British Land on a major regeneration project in Sheffield's River Don District. His other key clients include North East London Foundation Trust, University of Greenwich, ASDA, Land Securities, Royal Mail Group, PruPIM, Targetfollow, ISIS and National Grid.

Salary and other benefits

Actual rates of pay vary according to where you work and who you work for. As a guide, these are average pay rates:

- graduate starting salaries – around £24,000 a year
- average salary for a chartered surveyor – around £49,000
- top salaries – can be more than £100,000 a year.

Most surveyors receive additional benefits as part of their salary package. These may include performance-related bonuses and a company car.

Further information

- Royal Institution of Chartered Surveyors (RICS), RICS Contact Centre, Surveyor Court, Westwood Way, Coventry CV4 8JE. Tel: 0870 333 1600. Website: www.rics.org.
- *Careers 2011*, Trotman Publishing

CHAPTER 5

ARMED FORCES

An introduction to the armed forces

The armed forces offer officer training in the Army, Navy and RAF. These jobs are diverse and range from combat soldier to highly skilled engineer, pilot, medical or intelligence officer. Some roles are front line; others are supportive and may be largely office-based. All these roles demand high levels of fitness, personal integrity, courage and leadership. The recent events in Iraq and Afghanistan show clearly the real risk of personal injury and even death. This is not to frighten you off, but to make you aware of the unique position that you will find yourself in if you want to join the armed forces.

You need to ask some searching moral questions before joining. Would you be willing to go into a combat zone knowing that you may be asked to take action that would result in the death of another person? Do you have any religious objections? Would you be comfortable, as a Muslim for instance, fighting against other Muslims? This is a very real issue for Muslims in the military today.

A career in the armed forces is demanding but very rewarding; and it offers you world-class training in skills that are highly transferable once you leave. There is also the expectation that you will continue to acquire new skills once in the role. Professional development is vital to long-term success, so a willingness to combine the day-to-day demands of the job with evening or weekend study is important. The hours you work both in your day job and in your after-hours study are varied and the military involves long periods away from home.

Key skills for a career in the armed forces include:

- common sense, confidence and good communication skills
- integrity
- the ability to work under pressure, at times in situations that are very dangerous, and to command respect under pressure
- the ability to work as part of a team and on your own

- being quick-witted and able to solve problems swiftly and without too much help
- having clear leadership qualities
- being physically fit enough to undertake the duties expected of you. Part of the recruitment process for the armed forces involves assessing physical fitness and leadership qualities.

You must also be willing to undergo a vetting process that carefully checks the background of all applicants.

Army officer

What does an Army officer do?

The Army is one of the three branches of the armed forces, which protect the interests of British citizens both in the UK and abroad. It works closely with the other services (RAF and Navy) yet retains a distinct identity. The British Army also joins with other nations to protect NATO (North Atlantic Treaty Organisation) countries if they are attacked, and it is often called upon to undertake missions with the UN (United Nations).

The British Army has fought in many conflicts and is currently engaged in operations in Afghanistan. It maintains a presence in other parts of the world including Cyprus, the Falkland Islands and Iraq. Its soldiers enjoy a very high degree of respect worldwide for being highly motivated, disciplined and well-trained.

An Army officer leads a team of soldiers. As an officer you would lead combat operations and oversee the training, discipline, welfare and career development of the soldiers under your command.

The Army is made up of regiments and corps. Army officer jobs within these regiments and corps are broken down into four areas.

1. **Combat:** fighting regiments such as the Infantry who may be involved in engaging the enemy on the battlefield, peacekeeping, or delivering humanitarian aid.

2. **Combat support:** providing the combat regiments with direct support on the battlefield, in areas such as artillery and engineering, as well as indirect support, such as intelligence.
3. **Combat service support:** helping every part of the Army to function effectively, from maintaining its vehicles to ensuring the physical wellbeing of its personnel.
4. **Professionally qualified officers (PQOs):** personnel who qualified prior to joining the Army, including doctors, pharmacists, physiotherapists, dentists, nurses, veterinary surgeons, barristers and solicitors, and ministers of all faiths. These officers work across the Army, providing the same services to Army personnel as they would in civilian life.

The officer ranks in the Army are listed below, from the highest to the lowest:

- general
- lieutenant general
- major-general
- brigadier
- colonel
- lieutenant colonel
- major
- captain
- lieutenant
- second lieutenant
- officer designate.

Key skills required

- **Physical and mental fitness.** The Army expects a high level of personal fitness when you apply. As an officer you would take the Regular Commissions Board (RCB), which is a course that assesses your potential as an officer. Part of the course involves a test of your core fitness. Many applicants have to train hard to reach this basic standard in the weeks leading up to the RCB. In addition you would be expected to have mental toughness and a proven ability to cope in times of stress.

■ **Leadership and personal initiative.** The Army will look for evidence in your profile that you have led a group and taken some initiative. This might include leadership at Army Cadet level, Scouts, participation in the Duke of Edinburgh's Award scheme or any number of other pastimes that demand commitment and personal sacrifice.

■ **Good academic record.** Officers are normally, but not exclusively, graduates, but they come from a wide range of disciplines. Many undergraduates join the relevant University Officer Training Corps at university. In addition, as a disciplined uniformed organisation the Army expects an applicant to have a good moral compass with few, if any, significant brushes with the law! All applicants will face extensive police checks to ensure that they are suitable to work in a sensitive environment.

■ **Empathy** and the ability to work well with people from all walks of life.

■ **Tenacity, confidence, enthusiasm and humour** are also key skills that assessors look for.

Entry routes

The first port of call should be an Army recruitment centre. Many candidates are recruited from schools or universities via visits from the Army Careers Office.

The minimum age for recruitment is 17 years and nine months and the maximum age is 28. (This does not apply to the Medical Corps.)

The vast majority of applicants are graduates, but applications for officer training are also accepted from post-A level students. The minimum standard is two A levels and seven GCSEs graded A*–C.

Some regiments expect a certain type of degree; these include the Medical Corps, which expects you to have a suitable medical, dental or nursing qualification. Other regiments will find engineering, mathematics or a foreign language degree desirable.

If you are still doing GCSEs, you could apply for a place at Welbeck College. This is a defence forces sixth-form college, where all students study A levels and expect to join the military. In addition, the Army offers a limited number of sixth-form bursaries, undergraduate bursaries (engineering and medical, veterinary, nursing and dental sciences) and cadetships.

Full details of the above schemes are available at www.armyjobs.mod.uk/education.

Training and development

Most training takes place on the 48-week Commissioning Course (CC) at the Royal Military Academy, Sandhurst (RMAS). The course focuses on officership, command and leadership, and includes field training, physical training, weapons training and drill.

New army officers who hold professional qualifications follow the Professionally Qualified Officer (PQO) Course at RMAS, which lasts 10 weeks. This would apply, for instance, to a Medical Corps applicant.

After completing this initial training, new officers are commissioned and leave RMAS to begin specialist training in preparation for joining their chosen regiment or corps.

Continuing professional development (CPD) in the armed forces is common and regular. All young officers attend courses to learn the skills of their particular arm or service in preparation for their first command of a troop or platoon. These courses are designed to give you the confidence to command your soldiers and to improve your problem-solving, interpersonal and management skills. Further education is provided as appropriate to meet individual needs in future postings.

Job prospects

Promotion is offered on a merit basis and an officer would normally be expected to rise from the rank of second lieutenant to captain in three years. Promotion to major might take a further three to five years. Top-ranking officers should expect to have served for over 16 years before attaining these ranks.

Salary and other benefits

- Non-graduate officer cadets start on £15,268 a year.
- Graduate officer cadets start on £24,133.
- Captains earn between £37,172 and £44,206.

■ Salaries for higher ranks (from major to brigadier) range from £46,824 to £98,984.

The Army provides accommodation for both single and married officers and dependants, many kinds of leave, and free medical and dental care.

Further information

■ www.army.mod.uk
■ Army information pack and DVD from www.army.mod.uk or armed forces careers offices
■ Welbeck College, The Defence Sixth Form College, Forest Road, Woodhouse, Loughborough LE12 8WD. Tel: 0845 600 1483. Website: www.welbeck.mod.uk
■ www.camouflage.mod.uk (for 12–17-year-olds)

Royal Air Force (RAF) officer

What does an RAF officer do?

The RAF exists first to protect UK airspace and second to provide support to the Army and Navy during operations outside the UK. In addition, the RAF takes part in search and rescue operations both at sea (in collaboration with the coastguard) and on land (often in collaboration with the police). Another vital role is peacekeeping (sometimes as part of a UN force) and disaster relief, dropping off supplies and personnel where they are most needed. The RAF played a key role in the 2010 Haiti earthquake disaster relief project.

Although officers are based in the UK they may need to train abroad or take part in overseas missions. This can be disruptive to family life as you are often 'posted' to a base for a limited amount of time before moving on.

Officers are the senior managers of the RAF. They manage, lead and take responsibility for the welfare of the airmen and airwomen in their command. They also specialise in one of the following roles.

- **Pilots** are the best known members of the RAF. They train to fly both airplanes and helicopters. Some of the planes are fighter aircraft (such as the Tornado) and others are larger planes, e.g. Hercules and Nimrod. Helicopters transport troops or equipment. The Sea King helicopter is often used for sea and land rescue operations. Pilots are highly trained personnel and competition for places is intense.

- **Weapons systems officers** manage air-to-air combat in Tornado aircraft or operate weapons systems in other aircraft.

- **Engineer officers** specialise either as aerosystems engineers, responsible for the weapons, avionics and propulsion systems of all kinds of aircraft; or as communications electronics engineers, maintaining every type of communications link from telephone exchanges to satellite communications.

- **Catering officers** manage accommodation, restaurants and other eating areas, reception areas, bars and lounges. They also set up and manage catering in the field.

- **RAF police officers** lead the RAF's own police force.

- **RAF regiment officers** lead infantry units which defend RAF airfields and other installations from ground and low-level air attack.

- **Dental officers** are qualified dentists, practising on UK bases and overseas.

- **Medical officers** are qualified doctors, providing medical care for RAF personnel and their families.

- **Medical support officers** support the RAF's medical services in a range of management and administrative roles.

- **Personnel support officers** provide support services such as personnel management, accounting, estate management and public relations.

- **Chaplains** minister to the wider RAF community, including service families.

- **Legal officers** are qualified barristers and solicitors. They advise in criminal cases and conduct prosecutions both in the UK and overseas.

- **Physical education officers** arrange fitness programmes, organise adventurous training and run a wide range of sports facilities.

- **Training officers** design, set up and run training courses.

- **Air traffic control officers** use radar and communications equipment to help aircraft take off and land and provide pilots with flight and navigation information.

■ **Intelligence officers** obtain, analyse and provide defence intelligence.
■ **Supply officers** manage the movement of personnel, aircraft, freight, fuel, explosives and technical equipment.

The officer ranks in the RAF, from the highest to the lowest, are:

■ marshal of the air force
■ air chief marshal
■ air marshal
■ air vice marshal
■ air commodore
■ group captain
■ wing commander
■ squadron leader
■ flight lieutenant
■ flying officer
■ pilot officer.

Key skills required

■ **Physical and mental fitness.** The RAF is not a tough as the Army, but new recruits are expected to have a decent level of personal fitness. As an aspiring officer you would be assessed at the RAF HQ in Cranwell – this involves tests of both your mental and your physical fitness. Those wishing to join specific areas of the force, such as potential pilots or engineers, take additional tests to assess their suitability. Many applicants have to train hard to reach this basic standard in the weeks leading up to the assessment.
■ **Leadership and personal initiative.** The RAF will look for evidence in your profile that you have led a group and taken some initiative. This might include leadership at air cadet level, Scouts, participation in the Duke of Edinburgh's Award scheme or any number of other pastimes that demand commitment and personal sacrifice.
■ Applicants need a **sound academic record**, but there is no particular degree course that the RAF prefers. The exception to this would be if you are applying to become an aircraft engineer, in which case a professional qualification would put you at a distinct advantage. As with

all armed forces personnel, applicants need to be willing to go through positive vetting and police checks.

■ **Empathy** and the ability to work well with people from all walks of life.

■ **Tenacity, confidence, enthusiasm and humour** are also key skills that assessors look for.

Entry routes

Most officers are graduates; those who are not join the RAF after A levels. If you join the officer training course as a non-graduate, entry to many specialisations requires at least two A levels and five GCSEs (A*–C), including English and maths.

Some roles have more specific entry requirements:

■ engineer officers need a relevant degree or professional qualification

■ medical officers, nursing officers, legal officers and chaplains must be professionally qualified

■ dental officers can train as dentists with the RAF (this can be well worth doing as they pay while you train!) or can enter after qualifying

■ physical education officers need a relevant degree

■ training officers must have a degree or a professional qualification

■ catering officers need a relevant HND, degree or professional qualification.

All applicants must be British, Commonwealth or Irish citizens. For security reasons, there are stricter nationality requirements for some roles: for example, intelligence officers must have been British citizens since birth.

The RAF offers a range of sponsorship schemes for those in school sixth forms and at university. For more details look at the RAF Careers website or talk to an RAF recruitment officer at your school or college.

Applicants have to pass a series of selection tests held at the Officers and Aircrew Selection Centre at RAF College Cranwell in Lincolnshire. The selection process lasts for up to four days and includes aptitude tests, fitness assessments, interviews and an occupational health assessment.

Training

New entrants first take the 30-week initial officer training course. This does not apply to certain entrants, such as medical officers and legal officers, who undertake shorter training (around three months).

Further information is available at www.raf.mod.uk/careers. Applicants can also visit their local armed forces careers offices for further advice.

Job prospects

There are almost 9,000 officers in the RAF and this number is likely to remain static for the foreseeable future. Most officers join for between six and 12 years, with the option to extend that for many more if they wish. It is hard work and highly competitive to gain entry into the force, with entry to certain professions (such as pilot and navigator) being extremely competitive.

Salary and other benefits

An RAF officer joining the force as a graduate would earn in the region of £23,500 per annum as a pilot officer. This figure could be higher if you are a particularly well-qualified graduate. Promotion is based on competence. A middle-ranking officer will earn up to £43,000 and a more senior officer up to £60,000. If you already have a particular skill or qualification, such as in medicine or dentistry, the pay rates will vary according to your experience.

In addition, officers receive other benefits such as a good pension and accommodation at a reduced rate.

Further information

- www.raf.mod.uk
- RAF advice line: 0845 605 5555

Royal Naval officer

What does a Royal Naval officer do?

The Royal Navy is known as the 'senior service' because it is the oldest branch of the British military. From the beginning of the nineteenth century to the end of the Second World War, the British Navy was the largest navy in the world. In 1941 there were over 900 ships in the fleet. The role of the Navy has changed in the last 30 years, due in part to the end of the Cold War and the growing need for the Navy to patrol globally and be part of a rapid deployment force with air support capability in the form of aircraft carriers and helicopter ships. As of 2010, there were 87 commissioned ships in the Royal Navy, including:

- aircraft carriers
- a helicopter carrier
- landing platform docks
- ballistic missile submarines
- nuclear fleet submarines
- guided missile destroyers
- frigates
- mine counter-measures vessels
- patrol vessels.

As an officer in the Navy you will lead men and women both on board ship and in land-based naval stations. You will be expected to exhibit the highest levels of integrity and training as you undertake these duties. The role is diverse with a wide range of different branches, including medical, logistics or warfare. In these branches you might specialise in one of the following roles.

- **Aircrew:** includes working as a fast jet or helicopter pilot
- **Warfare:** these officers initially specialise in an aspect of a ship's operation. This might include mine warfare, fighter control or meteorology. Eventually these officers progress, on merit, to a position in which they might take control of a ship. (The submarine service is the only part of the Navy that remains a male-only domain.)
- **Engineering:** qualified officers work in weapon, marine or air engineering

- **Medical:** qualified doctors who work for the Navy
- **Air traffic control:** operate radar and the sophisticated communication systems that are a vital part of any ship or submarine.

The officer ranks in the Royal Navy are, from the highest to the lowest:

- admiral of the fleet
- admiral
- commodore
- captain
- commander
- lieutenant commander
- lieutenant
- sub-lieutenant.

Key skills required

- A high level of managerial ability and leadership.
- The ability to be decisive and take responsibility for your actions and decisions.
- The ability to work as part of a team.
- A good level of physical fitness, personal integrity and mental stability.
- Strong interpersonal and communication skills.
- A willingness to engage in activities that could be highly dangerous and stressful.
- A willingness to live at sea for months at a time with all that that entails for your social life.

Entry routes

Officers join as graduates in the majority of cases, although non-graduates may also enter officer training in the Navy if they have a minimum of five GCSEs (Grade A*–C) including English and maths plus at least 180 UCAS points from their A levels. For certain routes, such as medicine, dentistry or engineering, only graduates will be accepted.

Applicants must be British, Irish or Commonwealth citizens, with the exception of a few roles that are open to British citizens only. The Navy offers a limited number of scholarships for sixth formers and university students. If you are interested in one of these you should contact your local Navy careers office or speak to a naval careers officer if one visits your school. Full details can be found on the Navy website.

If you are successful in your paper application, you will be asked to attend a two-day residential assessment called the Admiralty Interview Board (AIB). This is held at HMS *Sultan* in Hampshire. It is rigorous and you need to make sure you are physically fit before you attend. If you wish to join aircrew you also need to pass the RAF flying aptitude tests at RAF Cranwell.

The AIB tests a number of things including fitness, numeracy, mental agility, written communication, oral communication, spatial awareness, knowledge of the Navy, leadership and emotional maturity. You will also be asked to plan and execute an exercise and undertake a one-to-one interview. A medical examination is also part of the test.

The maximum age of entrants is 25 for aircrew, 29 for engineers, 39 for chaplains and 46 for doctors.

Training and development

It takes a year to train as an officer and this training takes place at the Royal Naval officer training establishment, the Britannia Royal Naval College in Dartmouth. The training is diverse and includes fitness training, boat handling, leadership and management. You also undertake navigation training, meteorology, strategic studies, naval history and basic sea survival, and you will spend at least 10 weeks on board an operational ship.

Once you graduate you spend another three years in further training as you begin to specialise. You will sometimes be based on shore and sometimes off shore. Training is part and parcel of your life, so a willingness to continue to learn is vital.

Job prospects

There are around 6,500 officers employed in the Navy. The Navy aims to recruit around 500 officers a year and jobs are open to all, regardless of gender, religious belief or ethnic origin. The one exception is the Submarine Service, which only recruits male officers: this is because submarines have limited facilities and no room for separate female accommodation and bathrooms!

Officers are normally employed for a minimum of 12 years, with the option of extending this further. This does not apply to certain professional entrants, such as doctors, dentists and nursing officers. Naval officers are obliged to serve for a minimum of three to five years before they give notice (12 months) of their intention to leave before the end of their commissioned service. It is important therefore to have a very clear idea of what you are letting yourself in for!

Salary and other benefits

A graduate joining the Navy would expect to earn £29,000 as a sub-lieutenant. Promotion is based entirely on merit and as you are promoted, so your salary rises. A lieutenant can earn up to £44,000 and a captain in excess of £85,000. Senior ranks are paid over £100,000.

In addition, you receive cheap accommodation and other fringe benefits including a very good pension.

Further information

- www.royalnavy.mod.uk
- *Real Life Guide: The Armed Forces*, Trotman Publishing

CHAPTER 6

BANKING AND FINANCE

An introduction to banking and finance

A career in banking and finance is a varied and fascinating one and there are opportunities for employment all over the world. The three major world centres for banking and related industries are the City of London, New York and Tokyo. London is currently the number one centre because its location on the timeline means that it bridges the close of the Asian markets and the opening of the US markets. As a result, many of the world's banks and finance houses have offices in London. That being said, there are many UK finance jobs that are not based in London: finance professionals support businesses and individuals in towns and cities all over the UK.

All the major capitals of the world have stock exchanges and financial districts that offer employment in a diverse range of businesses. If you enjoy modern foreign languages you could work for a bank in Europe or further afield.

A career in finance can take many forms.

- **Insurance.** All individuals and companies need insurance to protect themselves against unforeseen events such as fire, theft or loss of earnings, so insurance is a vital part of the finance world. People tend either to work in a company offering insurance (insurance brokers, see p 49) or for organisations that offer to underwrite insurance policies (insurance underwriters, see p 47). The other major role is an actuary, who assesses risk. Those working in this profession tend to have high levels of mathematical competence. These jobs will be explained in more detail later in the chapter. A graduate with more or less any degree can apply, but you must have a decent level of numeracy.
- **Banking.** There are opportunities in a number of fields, including retail banking (this is essentially high street banking), investment banking, capital markets and stockbroking. Although employers look for able graduates from all backgrounds, applicants with a business, finance, mathematics and/or physics background tends to have an advantage.

DELOITTE

Name
Crystal Eisinger

University and degree
Cambridge – Social & Political Sciences

When did you join Deloitte?
September 2008

Why did you join the Deloitte scholar programme?
First and foremost I thought it would provide excellent work experience which would allow me to build a strong CV and gain early insight into the professional services industry. The second thing that attracted me to the programme was how financially rewarding it is, both during the gap year and throughout university. I wanted to join Deloitte specifically as it is a globally recognised and respected brand which made it a great place for me to start my professional career.

Which department/s have you worked in during the scheme
Tax: Tax Management Consulting : 9 months
Consulting: Public Sector, Strategy: 6 weeks
Financial Services Industry, Strategy: 6 weeks

Describe your experience to date of the scholar programme
My experience of the programme has been fantastic. I've had a wide variety of work during my gap year and an increased level of responsibility each time that I've returned for a placement. I've also found that social events and training programmes are a great way to meet people across the firm and to get to know colleagues outside of the office. I particularly enjoyed having the opportunity to get involved with community outreach programmes and scholar recruitment.

I've been involved in a diverse range of projects both in terms of the client and the nature of the work. I spent my gap year in Tax Management Consulting (Tax) and one of the projects that I was allocated to was a tax transformation project for a leading oil company. Upon returning for subsequent placements in Consulting I've rotated through different industries. For example I worked in Public Sector Strategy on an Economic Impact Assessment for a leading gaming and betting company and my latest placement has been in Financial Services Strategy, on a public sector pensions project which has been fascinating.

What do you feel are the benefits of taking part in a scholar scheme such as the one at Deloitte?
The benefits I've gained from the scholar scheme were both professional and personal. I've made a wonderful group of friends both with other scholars and people in the office. The scholar scheme guarantees paid work every holiday which is good for the bank account and the CV. The scholar scheme is so special because it allows you to grasp the scope of professional services and different industry areas before you apply for a graduate job. Being able to return whilst at university is particularly good because meaningful placements allow you to work in areas in which you are genuinely interested and begin to build a network of contacts in the professional services industry.

What does the future hold for you both at Deloitte and your career?
In the time between now and when I graduate I hope to do placements in different parts of the firm and after that I hope to join Deloitte as a Graduate. I feel that the programme has equipped me to go into any professional services environment and has been a great springboard for my future career.

■ **Accountancy.** This involves much more than adding up columns of figures. Accountants provide a broad range of advice to clients, who can be individuals, small businesses or international conglomerates. Accountants need to be well informed about the businesses they advise, and about the options available to their clients. All accountants need to have passed professional qualifications that are taken either as part of an accountancy degree or as a postgraduate qualification. Once again, a good level of mathematical competency is required.

INSURANCE

What does a person working in insurance do?

Insurance is one of the most important service industries in the UK, employing over 25,000 people. All of us use insurance, whether it is life assurance, holiday insurance or medical insurance. All companies, schools and other organisations need to have insurance and the policies they have will differ depending on the field of activity they are in.

People working in insurance tend to work in life assurance or general insurance. Life assurance is concerned with insuring individuals against premature death, ill health or permanent injury. Pensions insurance also falls into this category. General insurance is a broad term that covers all other aspects of the insurance business. This relates to damage to property, personal injury and other liabilities. It includes all forms of business insurance, some of which is highly specialised and requires particular skills or qualifications.

The third type of insurance is a specialist area called reinsurance. This is what insurance companies do to spread the risk of their own policies. They take insurance against getting large numbers of unforeseen claims – one possible reason for this could be after a major disaster when many people are claiming at once.

The two principal jobs you might choose to apply for are as an underwriter or a broker. There are others, for example claims, actuarial, risk management or investment analysis. However, for the purposes of this profile we shall focus on the first two.

LLOYD'S OF LONDON

Over 300 years ago Lloyd's started out in Edward Lloyd's coffee house as a place where people with exposure to risks could meet people with capital who, for a price, would agree to insure them. That's exactly what Lloyd's is today: a face-to-face market, with all the dynamism and imagination that a market generates.

Lloyd's is not an insurance company itself. It does not advertise for business in the way that insurance companies such as Zurich or Direct Line do.

It is a sort of modern-day coffee house where hundreds of different insurance companies 'meet' to spread the risk.

Entry routes

Most managerial positions in the insurance industry are held by graduates. They come from across the social spectrum and do not have to have any particular type of degree. If you are very keen to work in this industry it might be worth looking at a finance-based degree, but it is by no means vital.

Job prospects

The insurance industry, like all other financial service industries, has struggled in the recent recession. However, the signs are there now that graduate recruitment in the insurance sector is improving.

'The general insurance industry has been buoyant for the past few years, and confidence in the market for pensions and other savings products appears to be picking up,' says Steve Wellard, Communications Director at the Chartered Insurance Institute (CII).

'The big players – Prudential, Aviva and Legal & General – have all reported positive results, and it is expected they will re-invest their profits into their business, creating a need for more people.'

In the UK the major graduate employers include Alliance Trust, Royal & Sun Alliance (now RSA), Aviva, Lloyds Banking Group, Zurich and Prudential. There are dozens of smaller companies with graduate entry schemes.

Underwriter

What does an underwriter do?

An underwriter either works for an insurance company or is part of a syndicate at Lloyd's. An underwriter has a number of roles. First, they assess risks presented by clients. Then they evaluate the risk, working with an actuary, and decide if the risk is reasonable. If it is, they issue a policy, decide what conditions the policy should have and how much it should cost. What happens then is that the insurance company sells the policy to the client at a profit.

This illustration might help to explain this more clearly. Say you want to insure a building against fire damage. You go to an insurance company such as Direct Line and they contact an underwriter who decides whether the request is reasonable. The underwriter creates a policy to cover you for fire damage to your building. The insurance company then sells you the policy and adds a fee to make their profit.

Underwriting is about making crucial decisions that can have a direct bearing on the success of an insurance company. Underwriters arrange and authorise insurance policies with brokers or directly with customers.

A trainee underwriter has to learn to understand the risks associated with customers' daily lives and to help them manage those risks. There are many types of insurance policy, ranging from insuring the largest multinational businesses to individuals' houses and pets. In addition, underwriters have to build close relationships with customers to understand their needs.

According to the insurance company Royal & Sun Alliance, an applicant who wants to become an underwriter needs a good degree and must be a strong negotiator. You would also have to be up to speed on social, economic, legal and technological changes, ranging from issues such as climate change through to the very latest technology to evaluate the potential impact on insurance risks.

Key skills

- The ability to write clearly and logically, with an eye for detail, so that the policy has no ambiguities or errors.
- Numeracy – some but not all underwriters will have A level Maths.
- Good interpersonal skills.
- The ability to be discreet when handling sensitive material.
- A willingness to work on their own and in a team, showing appropriate leadership skills.

Training and development

All underwriters take professional exams after graduation. These can take up to four years to complete. They are designed and accredited by the Chartered Insurance Institute (CII) and the exams you take depend on the area of insurance that you specialise in. For instance, you can take exams related to claims or underwriting. The exams are hard and the courses are a mixture of evening classes, day release and evening work. Most companies pay the costs associated with these courses as part of their professional development budget.

Job prospects

Once qualified, many underwriters move into other core areas of insurance, including risk management and brokering. Others choose to specialise in reinsurance or become expert in a particular area of insurance such as aviation or oil. Such people become senior underwriters, ultimately taking on managerial responsibility for teams of junior underwriters.

Some underwriters move into the sales field, developing their relationship-building skills to meet sales targets for specific types of insurance. This area of work can be particularly lucrative, attracting target-related bonuses.

Salary

City firms pay more than those outside London. However, starting salaries are normally good, ranging from £25,000 to £30,000. As you progress, your earnings will rise and salaries in excess of £60,000 are commonplace.

Insurance broker

What does an insurance broker do?

An insurance broker works closely with their clients, who might range from individuals to major multinational companies, to ensure that they have appropriate insurance cover. The role requires a great deal of specialist knowledge and brokers tend to devote themselves to one area to develop the expertise they need.

Key skills required

- Good presentation and communication skills.
- The ability to create good working relationships with a variety of clients in a competitive market.
- Numeracy and good IT skills.
- A good eye for detail.
- An awareness of legislation and regulations that will affect the policies that they can offer.

Actuary

What does an actuary do?

Because they assess risk, an actuary is one of the key members of any insurance company. It is a highly mathematical discipline and only the best mathematicians tend to be recruited into this field of insurance. A maths degree is the normal minimum entry requirement for any firm recruiting actuaries.

At RSA, as is normally the case at other large insurance firms, graduates join one of the three main areas of actuarial work in general insurance:

- **capital requirements:** the team responsible for creating the complex financial models that are used to assess the risks the company faces from past and future business
- **pricing of general insurance products:** based on the risk of the product, a price for the insurance is fixed that meets the needs of the company and the client. This is one of the most competitive businesses in the world, so all companies are very price-conscious
- **reserving of claims:** this group of actuaries are heavily involved in calculating the reserves the company needs to make sure it can meet all claims.

Claims manager

What does a claims manager do?

The purpose of insurance is to protect you against unforeseen incidents. Claims managers deal with claims from individuals or companies looking to cover these unforeseen costs. Such claims might be related to travel, cars, personal injury, theft or fire damage. The range is vast and a claims manager tends to become a specialist in one particular area.

Claims managers are not expected to have any particular degree. Good interpersonal skills are vitally important.

BANKING

Investment banker

What does an investment banker do?

Investment banking covers a broad range of different jobs. However, there are two primary areas of business: corporate finance; and capital markets. Both have a front office and back office department. The front office essentially meets clients and manages their needs directly and the back office supports the front office but has little direct contact with customers. The back office is often referred to as 'operations' and it includes all the usual range of posts including marketing, human resources (HR), IT and compliance.

While researching this book I looked at a number of banks to gain an insight into what they look for in graduate applicants. One such bank is JP Morgan, an American bank with a large European presence. It is a huge organisation with over 70,000 employees and assets of over $2 trillion. The information contained in this profile is drawn partly from JP Morgan and partly from other banks that operate in the investment banking world.

Corporate finance

Corporate finance offers clients the opportunity to raise money to fund expansion or research and development. This is achieved by selling shares or bonds. The money raised is given to the client minus a fee.

Shares (or equity capital) are sold to investors. The company will then use that money to support its business. In return the investor gets a share in the company, which can be sold on the open market (via a stockbroker) at – hopefully – a profit. In addition investors are paid a dividend. This is a fixed sum of money per share owned. For instance, if you owned 10,000 Tesco shares and they pay a dividend of 15p per share, you would receive an annual payout of £1,500.

Companies also sell corporate bonds. These are called debt capital. Bonds are promises to pay both a fixed amount of interest for the life of a bond (say 3% per annum) plus the total value of the bond at the end. So, to take a simple example, if you bought a £10,000 Tesco corporate bond paying 3% for 10 years, you would receive 3% of £10,000 per year in interest and at the end of the bond's life get £10,000 back too. This is a safer way of making money, but very few individuals buy bonds. They tend to be bought by fund managers, who manage the money in pension funds or unit trusts. Fund managers might buy £10,000,000 worth of bonds and use the interest. The money raised helps a company pay its pensions. If you own a unit trust the value of the trust rises and so does your investment.

The great skill in this job is deciding the right price at which to pitch the share issue and when to issue bonds. Investment banks advise companies on this and, crucially, underwrite the sale. If the price is too high and no one buys the share/bond, the bank will pay the company anyway and lose money. Equally, if the shares sell well, the bank takes a cut of the profits and can make a lot of money.

Mergers and acquisitions

Mergers and acquisitions (M&A) is a key part of the investment banks' role in the City of London. M&A involves finding the right companies for a client to buy, merge with or indeed sell. Once this is established the M&A team arrange the deal. It is a highly lucrative part of the business as fees are high. As a result it is also highly competitive and risky for the bank. This area attracts some of the brightest and most ambitious graduates.

If two companies combine the deal is called a merger. If one company takes over another it is called a takeover. Some takeovers are mutually agreed and others are 'hostile' – when the company that is subject to the attention of the buyer does not want to sell. Often these mergers or takeovers involve household names. Recent mergers and takeovers include the merger of AOL and Time Warner in the USA and the foundation of the Lloyds Banking Group when Lloyds took over HBOS.

M&A deals comprise two stages. At the pitching stage the banker meets the clients, suggests strategies and researches the market to find out the best way forward. This is time-consuming and at times highly confidential as the price of a share can change drastically if rumours of an M&A get out. New entrants to the profession (they are called junior analysts) work to create the pitch book. This is the document containing all the information that the senior managers need to use when pitching the idea to their clients. It should be noted that many pitches come to nothing.

The second stage is the execution stage. This is when a target is agreed, the bank is engaged to work for the client and the transaction starts. This process is also time-consuming and involves working closely with lawyers, accountants and other professionals to ensure that the deal goes ahead.

The hours in this job can be very long indeed, and the industry is cut-throat: employees are only as good as their last deal.

Capital markets

Traders

Some of the most desirable jobs in investment banking are in sales and trading. This is the area that appears in most movies about the City. You are essentially a salesperson and you need to be articulate, quick-witted and happy to 'sell' on the phone or face to face.

You might find yourself trading equities (shares) (these people are called stockbrokers), bonds (bond dealers), foreign exchange (referred to as Forex dealers) or other commodities such as swaps or futures. You sell to traders at commercial banks, investment banks and large institutional investors (called fund managers). Trading can be hectic and requires a thorough knowledge of markets, financial instruments and an intuition for human psychology.

Equities trading positions often involve 'telling a story' to other traders about why they should purchase your stock. Derivatives traders need very strong analytical know-how (perhaps even an engineering degree). Foreign exchange trading is based more on your instincts about markets, politics and macroeconomics.

The job is stressful, cut-throat and not one suited to someone who lacks confidence in their own ability.

Fund managers

A fund manager looks after money held by pension funds, insurance companies, local councils, unit trusts and in some cases rich clients. Most specialise in a particular area, such as oil, automobiles or a particular geographical market. They work closely with investment analysts (who spend their time writing documents about different investment opportunities) and with other salespeople. Much of the job involves working closely with clients and essentially you are as good as your 'book'. If you make money for a client they will invest more – lose it and you will be out of a job!

Trainee fund managers have to take professional qualifications over and above their degree.

Key skills required

All the functions of the bank require the following broad key skills.

- A level of academic ability that will enable you to cope with the complexity of the business.
- Good numerical and IT ability.
- Willingness to work in a team in often stressful and competitive conditions.
- Evidence of personal ambition, leadership and energy.
- An ability to find solutions that may not be conventional or commonplace.
- Integrity.
- Good communication and presentational skills – you will be pitching to top management in multinational companies.
- Willingness to work long hours, sometimes overnight and into the weekend.
- Willingness to take a range of professional qualifications alongside your normal workload – this requires resilience and commitment.

Entry routes

There is no such thing as a standard entry requirement: graduates from all backgrounds, nationalities and academic disciplines are welcome to apply. In

Work experience?
No, it's life experience

Scholars Scheme

Deciding what to do with your life can be a daunting prospect. How do you know what's going to be right for you until you've tried it? Work experience is one option, but at Deloitte we know that it's life experience that's really important.

Our seven month gap year Scholars Scheme combines the best of both worlds, with paid employment, great experience, and a £1,500 travel bursary for you to travel anywhere you like to expand your horizons – not to mention four-week paid placements every year of university.

Are you ready for the experience of a lifetime? Take a look at **www.deloitte.co.uk/scholars** to find out more. **It's your future. How far will you take it?**

Deloitte.

Case study

Name: Mike

Job Title: Sponsored Undergraduate Technologist (SUT)

So, is your job too secret to tell us about?

"(Laughs) I get asked that a lot. Obviously, a good deal of the work we do is right at the forefront of technological development, but I still wait for my start-up scripts to run like any other programmer. At the moment I'm building a project with some tricky language processing techniques. I've spent a fair amount of time with some very, very clever people over the last month. But my mind is a bit of a sponge for that kind of stuff. I love learning."

So do you just like sitting and coding?

"I do enjoy it, but I actually enjoy the broader opportunities too. This morning, I went to a presentation given by an analytical area of GCHQ and I started thinking about how the tool I'm working on could have helped them. I prefer sitting in the sun in the courtyard, to sitting coding! I always get some fresh air at lunchtime. SUT's also get involved in helping out the new years' intake.

I had a quick chat yesterday with some other people who joined last year about organising a familiarisation event and a meal out in Cheltenham."

What is the social life like?

"I'm part of a fairly sociable team. And there's lots going on in the local area. My passion is football. I play regularly in an inter-departmental league – we're just avoiding relegation at the moment. Mainly as there isn't a lower league…"

What do you think about the company benefits?

"If I'm honest, I didn't really look into things like holiday entitlement when I was applying for jobs. I guess I was very lucky to get the job here! Now my friends are all working for software houses, I know how benefits can vary massively. We work hard at GCHQ, we enjoy the work, but it is important to have down time and enjoy a healthy work/life balance. I'm a very, very early riser, so I like to start work early. Not many companies can give you that kind of flexibility."

www.careersinbritishintelligence.co.uk

GCHQ

it's an interesting world

Look a little deeper.

Student & Graduate opportunities | Cheltenham | £competitive + benefits

IT, Internet, Engineering, Mathematics, Language and Culture Specialists

Sponsored Undergraduate Technologist scheme

Take a closer look at the world. Conflict, terrorism, military action and the increasing use of the internet are posing a growing number of threats to UK interests. As one of the UK's three intelligence and security agencies (alongside MI5 and MI6) we use the latest and most exciting technology to counter those threats, as well as providing world class advice and consultancy on information security issues to customers in government and industry.

At GCHQ our world-class training will prepare you for a successful career. As well as hundreds of opportunities for university graduates, we also take on school leavers to train in IT support or specialist careers in electrical and electronic engineering. And if you'd prefer to go to University, why not check out our Internships and Sponsorship opportunities? Whichever way you join us, you'll really get under the skin of world events. Help create a safer world by taking a closer look at *our* world of work.

www.careersinbritishintelligence.co.uk

Applicants must be British citizens. GCHQ values diversity and welcomes applicants from all sections of the community. We want our workforce to reflect the diversity of our work.

GCHQ

it's an **interesting** world

practice you will need to be a strong candidate with a good academic profile. Not Oxford or Cambridge – that idea is now long gone; but you will need a good degree and a solid A level performance.

Some degrees are more helpful than others and applicants with a maths/ business/financial degree will have an advantage, at least in the short term. That being said, BarCap (the capital markets division of Barclays) employed more physics and engineering graduates than graduates from any other subject in 2009. They did so because physics combines maths and problem solving – often an important skill in an investment bank.

Job prospects

London is full of banks that are looking to recruit bright young graduates to join their profession. Competition is fierce but if you are good you could become very successful, and very rich too. However, you are only as good as your last trade or project. As such, job security is not high and many people leave their jobs to be replaced quickly by others.

If you are employed by a bank the size of JP Morgan, for example, you could expect to be offered many different opportunities, including time spent working overseas. For many young people this is the attraction of working for a multinational organisation. Banks offer continuing professional development (CPD) and all employees wanting to progress have to work hard at CPD to win the promotions they want.

Salary

Your starting salary will depend on which part of investment banking you join. However, starting salaries in London firms are generous and often exceed £30,000 per annum. Your salary will increase from then on and with bonuses could easily exceed £70,000 per annum. Traders have the most to earn in terms of bonuses and sometimes these can exceed their basic salary. Be warned, though: competition is fierce and the bank will sack anyone who fails to meet their targets.

Further information

■ *Careers 2011*, Trotman

High street or retail banking

What does a retail banker do?

When you walk down the high street of any town or city you will see retail banks. The big four are Lloyds Banking Group, RBS/NatWest, HSBC and Barclays. A high-profile new arrival in the UK is Santander, a Spanish banking giant that has bought a number of smaller banks and building societies in the UK.

A retail bank is a bank whose primary business is the day-to-day needs of ordinary individuals and small to medium-sized companies. They look after millions of customers' current accounts (bank accounts that are for normal daily use) and deposit accounts (for savings), and provide mortgages to help you buy a house and insurance to protect you if disaster strikes. These are the banks that you see on the high street.

Lloyds, Barclays and their like all have non-retail banking departments too, but their primary business is retail rather than corporate or investment banking. The retail banking world has changed a lot in recent years, not helped by the banking crisis that enveloped the world in 2007/8. They now face fierce competition from e-banking and new players in the market, including supermarkets, who now offer a range of products suitable for individuals.

While the banking sector has been consolidating, it is worth noting that far more people have jobs in the retail banking sector than any other part of the financial services industry. Jobs in retail banking can be exciting and offer excellent opportunities.

Today's retail banks are more diverse than ever. You'll find a tremendous range of opportunities, from the branch level, where you might start out as a cashier, to a wide variety of other services such as leasing, credit card banking, international finance and trade credit.

When conducting research into this profile I focused on one well-known UK bank, the Lloyds Banking Group. Lloyds Banking Group offer graduate programmes that are similar to many other banks, so the information below is useful whichever bank you join.

For graduate entrants the role of a bank manager remains a prime choice, but other areas of interest may include the following.

- **Marketing and public relations (PR)** promotes the bank, through the media, in a crowded and competitive market. This area would appeal to someone who is interested in marketing, media relations, PR and advertising.
- **Credit risk** is a specialist position that assesses all forms of risk to a bank and recommends appropriate lending. All banks lend money at a risk. If you borrow £10,000 to buy a car, it is on the understanding that you are capable of paying back the money. If you do not, the bank loses that money and its profits fall. Poor lending to people unable to manage the debt was a prime cause of the recent banking collapse.
- **Human resource management (HRM)** is a specialist position that deals with all aspects of employee relations including recruitment, promotion, terms and conditions, complaints, disciplinary proceedings and staff training.
- **Operations management** researches new operational opportunities and methods in order to get costs down and recruit more customers. For instance, the current move away from cheques as a means of payment towards chip and pin debit cards is something that an operations manager will be heavily involved with.

Key skills required

- A sound level of mathematical competence. This means that you must be numerate, but you do not necessarily need to have a maths degree.
- Excellent oral and written communication skills. You will be presenting bank policy not only internally but also in a competitive external environment to potential or existing customers.
- Ability to work as part of a team or on your own, depending on your role.
- Demonstrable leadership skills.
- An eye for detail.
- Good personal organisational skills and the ability to think analytically.
- Personal integrity – you will be working with confidential information.
- Ability to think creatively.

■ Ability to work in a busy, sometimes stressful environment where long hours are not uncommon.

■ Competence in a foreign language is increasingly useful.

■ Good IT skills.

Credit analysts are also expected to have: a high level of mathematical competence (A level Maths is a requirement for Lloyds Banking Group if you are a graduate entrant); strong IT competence, because so much work is done using complex software; and a willingness to learn the law relating to the lending they are assessing.

Entry routes

The main routes into retail bank management are through a graduate management training scheme or by internal promotion from a non-graduate scheme. Graduates normally need at least a 2:2 degree, but top banks would expect a 2:1 or better. Banks may consider any degree subject, but subjects such as accounting, mathematics, business studies, economics, finance and management are most relevant.

One course that you might want to consider is the BSc in Banking and International Finance offered by Cass Business School at City University London. However, there are a number of excellent banking courses out there and Cass is not necessarily the best fit for you. Some other well-respected courses are offered by Birmingham, City, Essex, Lancaster, Loughborough, Newcastle and Surrey universities. You would be well advised to look at all these universities as part of your research. Some offer degrees that are part-sponsored by banks who may offer to pay part of your fees. This is an attractive prospect, so look carefully when your time comes at what is being offered.

Any banking and finance degree will equip you with the academic knowledge to operate in the increasingly competitive world of financial markets. Employers in this sector demand graduates who are capable of analysing and solving complex problems in banking and finance, and who possess the ability to apply the principles of financial management in their work.

Applicants must normally have a minimum of an A in GCSE Maths and most also have maths at AS or A2. The entry standard is generally AAB or the equivalent. However, each university has slightly different expectations, so do your research carefully before deciding. Again, the best place to start is the UCAS website course search at www.ucas.com.

GRADUATE ENTRY SCHEMES

All the major high street banks have graduate entry schemes that are designed to encourage undergraduates to join them. Lloyds Banking Group operates a number of schemes to engage potential graduate entrants. These schemes are similar to others offered by competitors.

Internships

Internships are growing in popularity, due in part to the influence of the practice in the USA. Lloyds Banking Group offers highly competitive 10-week and 12-month internships to undergraduates. All other major banks – HSBC, Santander, Barclays and the American banks mentioned in the Investment Banker section above – offer internships. They are broadly similar in scope to the Lloyds Bank scheme. If you are keen to do an internship you need to get in touch with all the major banks once you start your undergraduate programme. Some UK banks also offer summer work placements for A level students. Details of these can be found on the banks' websites.

The Lloyds 10-week internship is taken during the long summer holiday and involves a placement in one of five areas of banking: corporate markets, finance, IT, business management or human resources. You choose one area that matches your interests and apply online. You are then assessed and if you are chosen you start an internship the following summer.

The 12-month internship is usually taken as a year out during an undergraduate programme. Most universities are happy to allow this. Lloyds offer a wide range of 12-month placements specifically designed to give students in their penultimate year of study a good understanding of the banking business and, in particular, how Lloyds Banking Group operates. This is a good opportunity to gain some work experience while simultaneously bolstering your CV, and allows you to decide whether a career in banking is definitely for you.

(Continued on the following page)

Graduate entry programme

All the major banks offer graduate entry programmes. The details differ from bank to bank, but they are essentially very similar. For details, go online and search for graduate entry programmes. You normally apply during your final year at university. (Once again, we are using the Lloyds Banking Group as an example but this information is as useful to anyone applying to any bank.) Graduate entrants joining Lloyds Banking Group apply for a place on one of five programmes, which are similar to the internship programmes, the difference being that this is a full-time job. The programme you choose will depend on your academic qualifications, interests and potential. Entrants complete an application form and then go through a range of interviews, psychometric tests and assessment centre exercises before they are admitted to the bank.

Job prospects

After the recent recession when many jobs were lost, the employment situation was pretty dire. The good news is that all the major banks are now recruiting again and reinstating their graduate employment schemes. Job prospects are likely to continue to improve. What is clear however is that the market is competitive and promotion in this profession is now based solely on your performance not your background. If you meet targets and work hard then you can rise to the top of the profession in a reasonable time frame. Graduates can expect to be managing departments and branches in their mid-thirties.

Salaries

Salaries depend on your level of entry and qualifications. However, as a general rule of thumb a new graduate entrant would expect to earn around £20,000, rising to over £25,000 in some larger banks. Salaries after that can rise sharply, with senior retail bank managers earning in excess of £100,000.

Further information

- *Inside Careers Guide to Banking, Securities and Investments*, Inside Careers.
- *Real Life Guide: Business, Administration and Finance*, Trotman Publishing
- *TARGETjobs City and Finance 2010*, GTI.

CHAPTER 7

CIVIL SERVICE

An introduction to the Civil Service

The Civil Service is an impartial, non-political organisation whose role is to support the government of the day and help them to deliver their policies across the whole range of government departments. It is divided into three main organisations – departments, agencies and non-governmental bodies. Civil servants can work on projects that touch upon all areas of government activity, from education to defence, health to work and pensions. All the well-known government departments in Whitehall have a team of highly skilled civil servants supporting the minister or secretary of state. In addition to those based in London, there are civil servants working throughout the UK in every town and city. In fact, of 500,000 employees, only 25% work in London.

There are a lot of graduate opportunities in the Civil Service and some of the brightest and most ambitious young people in the UK apply to work there every year.

The Civil Service is trying hard to break down the myths that surround the organisation: you do not need to be white and middle class to get on; and the days when the Oxbridge college you went to played a part in the interview process have gone. These days anyone from any background can join. They want talent, ambition and cultural diversity to match the nation. If you are up for it, they want to hear from you!

One of the ways they are working to recruit new people from outside the 'traditional' intake is through the Summer Internship Programme; and the Civil Service Summer Diversity Internship Programme for black and ethnic minority and disabled students was established with the aim of providing high-calibre undergraduates/graduates with a six- to nine-week stretching work placement in a government department. Both programmes are a perfect way to gain real-life experience of how departments function, the policy areas they are responsible for and how their work impacts on the public. The programmes will expand your horizons and help you make an informed choice about whether you are suited to the Civil Service and are genuinely motivated by the work. The key objectives of the programmes are to break down stereotypes that people still have about the Civil Service, and to give you an insight into the enormous range of opportunities on offer in the Civil Service with the hope that you will join the Civil Service fast stream and/or seek wider Civil Service opportunities.

A recent graduate of an internship programme is Roxanne Ohene, who had an internship with the Department for Education.

CASE STUDY: ROXANNE OHENE, CIVIL SERVICE INTERN

Roxanne has a BSc in Psychology from the University of Warwick and an MSc in Work Psychology and Business from Aston Business School. She was an intern on the Summer Diversity Internship Programme over the summer of 2002: she worked in the Department for Education and Skills (DfES, now the Department for Education) in the ICT Schools Directorate. Working in DfES gave her an excellent insight into the work of government, the role of civil servants and the opportunities available in the Civil Service fast stream.

As a result of her experience in the programme, Roxanne successfully applied to the Civil Service fast stream. She started her career in the Home Office, where she undertook a variety of roles including working in the ministers' private offices as a policy adviser and as a project manager. She spent two and a half years in the Prime Minister's Delivery Unit, where she worked in the Cabinet Office and subsequently HM Treasury. She worked to improve delivery on a wide range of home affairs areas including immigration, prisons, criminal justice and crime.

Roxanne is currently the Head of the Ministerial Delivery Unit in the Department for Business, Innovation and Skills (formerly the Department for Innovation, Universities and Skills (DIUS)), supporting ministers and the board to drive delivery of its priorities.

Civil Service Executive Officer

What does a civil servant do?

The Civil Service is one of the UK's leading employers with offices throughout the whole of the UK. Currently more than 500,000 people work for the service and these posts are spread across the whole country. Not all the jobs in the Civil Service are strictly professional in a conventional sense (although many are), and it is a career option that offers a huge range of opportunities to a confident and successful employee.

You could find yourself working in a variety of different departments, ultimately reporting to the senior politicians who make up the cabinet. You could work for HM Revenue & Customs, which essentially collects tax and looks after the entire UK government spending requirement; or you could work for the departments responsible for education, health, defence, the environment, justice, welfare or transport. Not all entrants to this career are graduates, indeed most are not, but a growing number are graduates and certainly senior civil servants who work closely with the prime minister and his or her team are professionals with degrees and postgraduate qualifications.

An executive officer is essentially a junior manager – they have different titles depending on what part of the government they work for – but they all have similar duties, which might include the management of a team, training, staff appraisals, meeting members of the general public, giving presentations and undertaking research projects for government ministers.

Key skills required

Some skills may be specific to a department, for instance accountancy qualifications. However all officers would be expected to show evidence of:

- management and leadership skills
- integrity – much of the work may be sensitive or confidential
- attention to detail
- competent IT and communication skills

- an ability to work on their own and in teams, often with tight deadlines to meet
- willingness to continue to learn on the job and acquire specialist skills to meet the needs of their managers.

Entry routes

Entry requirements differ from department to department. Increasingly, many departments do not specify any formal qualifications: they judge applicants against the competencies, skills and experience required for the job.

Some departments and agencies offer opportunities for undergraduates to undertake student placements and work experience; further details are on the Civil Service jobs website. There are also opportunities for day visits. Some government departments offer their own graduate recruitment schemes.

As well as completing an application form and attending an interview, candidates may be required to take a range of tests assessing numeracy, writing, communication and interpersonal skills, along with decision-making and analytical skills.

Graduates with at least a 2:2 honours degree in any discipline who can demonstrate the potential to become excellent negotiators and managers may apply to the Civil Service fast stream.

Fast Stream Accelerated Promotion Scheme

Certain graduates with particular potential are able to apply for the Civil Service fast stream. This is an accelerated training and development graduate programme. For this scheme, the Civil Service tends to look for graduates with at least a good 2:1 honours degree (in any subject) and competition for places is fierce.

The scheme offers successful applicants the chance to work in a variety of different departments. These postings last for 12 to 18 months. You tend to work on a particular project in each department and your progress is monitored carefully. Some applicants are lucky enough to be posted abroad, particularly if they have an interest in the Diplomatic Service.

Job prospects

The majority of civil servants work for one of four key departments – Defence, Welfare, HM Revenue & Customs or Work and Pensions. All jobs have a nationality requirement and are open to UK nationals or those with dual nationality if one part is British. Around 75% of jobs are also open to Commonwealth citizens and nationals of the European Economic Area.

Departments also carry out security checks through the Criminal Records Bureau (CRB) and other checks, such as health checks, prior to appointment.

Salary and other benefits

The starting salary for an executive officer is around £21,000 a year rising to £28,000 based on experience. Promotion to more senior positions can mean an increase in salary to over £35,000. All London-based Civil Service employees also receive an additional allowance which will boost their basic salary.

The Civil Service also offers a benefits package, including a pension scheme, to its employees. Depending on where employees work, there may be sports and social facilities or a subsidised cafeteria.

Further information

- www.civilservice.gov.uk
- www.direct.gov.uk
- Government Skills, Kingsgate House, 66–74 Victoria Street, London SW1E 6SW. Tel: 020 3300 8977. Website: www.government-skills.gov.uk
- National School of Government, Sunningdale Park, Larch Avenue, Ascot SL5 0QE. Tel: 01344 634000. Website: www.nationalschool.gov.uk
- *The Civil Service Year Book*, Stationery Office
- *How to Pass the Civil Service Qualifying Tests: The Essential Guide for Clerical and Fast Stream Applicants*, Kogan Page

CHAPTER 8

ENGINEERING

An introduction to engineering

Engineers work in a variety of different contexts, including building and construction, materials science, chemicals, and hardware and software development. Engineers are involved in the design and development of buildings, factory production machines, aircraft, tunnels, 3D television screens and sports clothing; they are also involved in solving bigger problems such as maintaining clean water and energy supplies and reducing pollution. Engineers use their knowledge of physics, maths and engineering, plus the product itself, to provide a client with what they want. Some engineers are solely involved in construction: these projects can vary from small-scale road-widening schemes to huge projects such as the construction of the Channel Tunnel, Olympic stadium and high-speed rail networks. All these projects need engineering experts to work alongside architects, planners and builders.

There are a number of different branches of engineering and one of the problems a potential engineer has is choosing which one to go into. The major branches are:

- civil engineering – the design and construction of dams, bridges, roads and canals and other structures that enhance the environment in which we live
- automotive engineering – the design and manufacture of cars and other vehicles
- electrical engineering – the design and manufacture of electronics, IT hardware, communication systems and power stations
- aerospace engineering – the design of aircraft and space technology
- mechanical engineering – the design of components, machines and systems that involve the conversion and use of mechanical energy
- chemical and materials engineering – converting natural resources to products such as paint, dyes, foods and perfumes
- marine engineering – the design of marine craft and structures (such as oil rigs)

■ renewable energy engineering – a new branch focusing on ways in which we can harness energy from renewable sources such as solar power, wind turbines and waves.

Around 1.5 million men and women work in engineering-related jobs in the UK and the sector is currently undergoing a massive transformation as it comes to terms with changes in the global economy and some of the cost advantages available in developing countries. However, engineering and engineering design is central to all developing technologies and people with the right skills will always be in demand.

A level students thinking about a career in engineering will need to have a strong science and maths background, as well as an interest in solving problems and creating new design solutions. Interestingly enough, engineering graduates who do not become full-time engineers are valued by other industries and employers as they often want people who are both numerate and skilled at solving problems.

Engineering can be taken as a subject in school or college. For example, the Diploma in Engineering can provide the first step towards college/university entrance.

Maths and physics are also important subjects, especially for those wanting to train to become engineers. Most university courses in engineering look for both maths and physics at A2, and some will also ask for chemistry.

One well-known engineering company that employs graduates is Arup, a global firm of designers, engineers, planners and business consultants that provides a diverse range of professional services to clients all over the world. It employs civil, structural and industrial engineers as well as architects and planners. If you worked for Arup you might find yourself building a new hospital, school, bridge, tunnel or football stadium. The company recruits more than 100 graduates a year (more details about their scheme are found in the civil engineering profile, on the next page).

There isn't room to discuss all the different types of engineering in this chapter, so we shall focus on civil engineering and electrical engineering. If you want to find out about the other fields of engineering, take a look at the Enginuity website (www.enginuity.org.uk).

A good source of information for those looking to do work placements in the engineering industry is Year in Industry (YINI), which offers placements to students before they go to university so that you can get a taste of what working in the engineering sector is like.

There is also Headstart, a company that organises taster courses for students who are thinking about engineering but aren't sure. This is well worth looking at if you are thinking of taking engineering at university.

Civil engineer

What do civil engineers do?

A civil engineer designs, builds and maintains the environment we live in. Whether it's road construction, railway maintenance, sea defences, power supply systems or building football stadiums, you will find a civil engineer at the heart of the process. Companies that employ civil engineers will bid for projects: this means that they put together a proposal to a client (say Arsenal Football Club) and suggest how they can build a new stadium (such as the Emirates) efficiently and at a cost that beats their rivals. If the client accepts the proposal, the civil engineer begins to turn it into a reality, working closely with others from the start of the project through to completion. That may take a long time in the case of a large project such as the Channel Tunnel, where construction took years and involved engineers from multiple branches, who at times were working at the cutting edge of technology.

Most civil engineers do specialise: some work on structures (tunnels, dams, roads); others prefer environmental projects (flood barriers, canals and renewable energy); or transport (roads, rail); maritime (sea and river defences – not ships); or geotechnical (mining and tunnelling).

In total 48,000 people work as civil engineers in the UK.

Key skills required

- Excellent IT skills.
- Creativity and an aptitude for problem solving.
- A good eye for detail.

- Good communication skills – you will work with people across many trades and professions.
- The confidence to work with numerous people and present ideas to groups.
- Willingness to work hard in sometimes arduous or dangerous conditions.
- Willingness to embrace unsocial working hours from time to time.
- Willingness to travel away from home, sometimes for an extended period, when working on a project.
- An interest in design, trends and current ideas.
- Willingness to learn and follow the many legal and regulatory rules that govern the profession.
- A sound eye for accounting and budgets.

Entry routes

In order to become a chartered civil engineer, you will need to take a degree course at a university that is accredited by the relevant Institute of Engineers. Alternatively, you could enter the profession through an Apprenticeship, gain engineering technician status, and progress to higher education from there if you wanted to. For more information about Apprenticeships, have a look at the Apprenticeships website (www.apprenticeships.org.uk).

There are many good degree courses and you would be well advised to look first at your local university to see what they offer. Degree courses provide excellent preparation, in terms of knowledge, understanding and key transferable skills, for a career in civil engineering. Many courses are fully accredited by the Institution of Civil Engineers and the Institution of Structural Engineers, providing the first stage in a recognised career path to chartered or incorporated engineer status. Employment prospects are excellent once you graduate.

Clearly it would be impossible to describe all the courses available, so what I have done here is focus on one course that I came into contact with when writing this profile. It is a good example of a standard civil engineering degree course and shares many of the features that you would find in similar universities. The information is specific to the University of Southampton, but useful for anyone looking to see if they have what it takes to succeed as an engineer.

The essential skills Southampton look for are numeracy, problem-solving ability and logical thinking. Therefore access to this course (and most other engineering courses) demands A level maths and a science (preferably physics), or equivalent qualifications. They also look for good communication skills, both written and oral. Other positive attributes are IT skills, a practical hands-on attitude to situations, and a flair for design and creativity, particularly for the civil engineering with architecture course.

Important personal qualities Southampton seeks in a potential professional engineer are: teamworking skills and leadership ability; and evidence of potential (for which they focus on a candidate's personal statements, describing sporting activities, clubs, societies, hobbies, voluntary activities or business games in which they have been actively involved).

Training and development

One leading engineering firm I contacted in researching this book is Arup. Although the information given below is specific to Arup, most of it is general enough to provide you with an insight into what all good engineering companies are looking for.

GRADUATE RECRUITMENT

Employers such as Arup have graduate recruitment programmes that recruit able young graduates with a desire to work for a major company. Arup recruits over 100 graduates in the UK each year. Other large firms employ similar numbers: smaller firms might only recruit a handful. You have to decide whether you would prefer to work for a large or small firm.

Each graduate at Arup is recruited with the stated intention of providing them with the opportunity to follow an appropriate training scheme to professional qualification. The majority of the 20 or so electrical engineering graduates they recruit each year will follow the Institution of Engineering and Technology scheme. This would be similar in all other major firms.

For all companies, including Arup, continuing professional development (CPD) is the key to success. Most graduates joining Arup will have

(Continued on the following page)

reached an academic standard appropriate for progression to CEng under the UK Standard for Professional Engineering Competence (UK-SPEC), but recruits with bachelor's degrees will be encouraged and supported to undertake work-based further learning, if applicable, towards achieving the highest possible level of professional qualification.

Graduates work on real, fee-earning projects from the start of their employment. Most learning is provided on the job and supplemented by internal or external secondments and training courses in technical, interpersonal and management skills.

Job prospects

The economic downturn has had a major impact on engineering companies. When money is tight, buildings do not get built, road programmes are delayed and as a result other projects can be put back or cancelled. Many engineers lost their jobs in 2008, but now that the economy is picking up, jobs are now being advertised again. However, most graduate recruitment schemes are still taking fewer graduates than before.

Salary

The average starting salary for a graduate is between £25,000 and £28,000 per annum. This will of course depend on the size of the firm you join. As you progress into middle management, salaries can rise to over £40,000 and chartered civil engineers earn considerably more.

Further information

- ■ Institution of Civil Engineers (www.ice.org.uk)
- ■ Arup (www.arup.com)
- ■ University of Southampton, School of Engineering Sciences (www.southampton.ac.uk/ses)
- ■ *New Civil Engineer* (www.nce.co.uk)
- ■ *Construction News* (www.cnplus.co.uk)

Electrical engineer

What does an electrical engineer do?

This is a branch of engineering that specialises in the development, production and maintenance of electrical machinery and equipment. Electrical engineers might find themselves working for a power or water company, working to produce more efficient means of generating and distributing power to homes and businesses. They could work for a company that is developing new methods of generating power from renewable sources, such as solar power, wind turbines and wave power. Others might specialise in systems designed to reduce pollution from power stations to reduce carbon dioxide output.

Electrical engineers also work on the production of all types of electrical equipment and machinery. There are therefore employment opportunities in a wide range of business in areas as diverse as food production, IT, tele-communications and the manufacture of components for military equipment. This is a research and development (R&D) role and often requires creativity, as you will be working at the cutting edge of modern technology. One unusual employer looking for expertise in this field is GCHQ, a part of the security services that works closely with MI5 and MI6. (Further details of their role can be found in Chapter 14.)

Many industries rely heavily on electrical engineers, including manufacturing and the transport industry (railways, ships, aircraft and road vehicles). Electrical engineers are vital in the development of communications, radar and instrumentation systems.

Professional electrical engineers are usually either incorporated or chartered. The majority of graduate entrants to the profession will work towards chartered status. Chartered engineers have a more strategic role, planning, researching and developing new ideas, and streamlining management methods; and are more likely to have managerial responsibilities.

Key skills required

The key skills that electrical engineers should have are broadly similar to those required of all engineers:

- an analytical mind
- strong mathematical skills
- willingness to work with all types of people, sometimes in hazardous environments
- good problem-solving skills
- IT literacy
- full colour vision.

Entry routes

You can enter the electrical engineering profession either through an Apprenticeship leading to engineering technician status or by studying for an accredited degree, which can lead to chartered engineer or incorporated engineer status after some work experience. Apprenticeships can also lead to higher education and degree study at a later date. For more information about Apprenticeships have a look at the Apprenticeships website, www. apprenticeships.org.uk.

All chartered or incorporated engineers must have a degree. There are many universities that offer relevant courses. One such university is the University of Birmingham. Their MEng course follows a very similar pattern to other courses on offer elsewhere in the UK, and this insight into the course will provide you with useful information whichever university you decide to apply to.

Birmingham has a three- or four-year programme that leads to a MEng in Electronic and Electrical Engineering. This programme provides a thorough overview of electronic technology and a solid grounding in underlying physical and mathematical principles. You learn about all levels in design, from transistors, transmission media and electromagnetic devices through to the organisation and control of large-scale systems such as computers, communication networks and transport infrastructure. This degree is ideal if you enjoyed mathematics and science at school and are seeking to develop and apply those subjects. Standard entry requirements for 2011 were ABB/ AAB with a C in Maths GCSE. Mathematics and physics to A2 is expected.

Job prospects

The economic downturn has hit all engineering firms. However, as the economy recovers there will be more opportunities for new graduates. At present, on average over 65% of electrical engineers gain a job within six months of completing their degree. The vast majority of the rest are engaged in further study, working part time or taking time out. The main reason to be confident is that engineering is a discipline whose skills are transferable. Other industries and employers value highly the problem-solving and numeracy skills held by engineers, so there should be other options open to you should you decide not to work in an engineering role.

Salary

The salary you earn will depend on the company you work for. However, as a rule of thumb, graduates starting with a company such as Balfour Beatty can expect to earn around £22,000 per annum rising to over £35,000 in a few years. Experienced chartered engineers earn in excess of £50,000 per annum.

Further information

- Engineering Council UK, 246 High Holborn, London WC1V 7EX. Tel: 020 3206 0500. Website: www.engc.org.uk
- Institution of Engineering and Technology, Michael Faraday House, Stevenage SG1 2AY. Tel: 01438 313311. Website: www.theiet.org
- SEMTA (Sector Skills Council for Science, Engineering and Manufacturing Technologies), 14 Upton Road, Watford WD18 0JT. Tel: 01923 238441; learning helpline: 0800 282167. Website: www.semta.org.uk
- WISE (Women Into Science, Engineering and Construction), 2nd Floor, Weston House, 246 High Holborn, London WC1V 7EX. Tel: 020 3206 0408 Website: www.wisecampaign.org.uk
- *Careers 2011*, Trotman Publishing

CHAPTER 9

HEALTHCARE PROFESSIONS

An introduction to the healthcare professions

Medicine is a science, an art and a profession concerned with the study and practice of human healing. People practising medicine understand human health and disease and are able to help patients with illness, whether it is through cure or maximising quality of life. Doctors are the first port of call for most people when they have a health-related problem, and it is the responsibility of the doctor to deliver the best all-round care possible to maximise every patient's health. However, doctors cannot do this alone, which is when other health professionals are called upon. These include the following.

- **Nurses** implement much of the care that is directed by doctors but they can also work independently of doctors. Broadly, doctors have overall responsibility for patients' care and are able to make diagnoses and prescribe treatment (although some nurses are now permitted to diagnose and prescribe for some conditions), while nurses are more patient-focused, spend more time with patients and are able to deliver much more holistic care than doctors. It could be said that nurses are the limbs and doctors are the eyes and brain of the core health service.
- **Dentists** specialise in the care of the teeth, mouth and jaw. Dentists often specialise in one area (e.g. surgery, orthodontics, paediatrics). Most dentists work privately rather than as part of the National Health Service (NHS). In general, they work independently of doctors, but there is often an overlap in the conditions they treat and the care they provide.
- **Allied health professionals** support the work of doctors, nurses and dentists in diagnosing and treating patients. There are many different professions within this subcategory, such as physiotherapists, dieticians, medical interpreters, speech and language therapists, radiographers, and pharmacists.

Every member of the health service plays a fundamental role in delivering care to patients, and all are vital members of the whole healthcare team. It is important that the best, most appropriate care is delivered to every patient, so a tailored and holistic approach is necessary. This care may be delivered by health professionals in a hospital, but can also take place in GPs' surgeries, day care centres, hospices and sometimes in the patient's home.

Around 1.7 million people work in healthcare in England, and jobs are available throughout the UK. The NHS is the largest single employer in the UK and offers over 300 different careers. Other healthcare employers include private, charitable and voluntary organisations, local authorities, the armed forces and the prison service. Whatever sector of health delivery medical professionals work in, their role is vital in making a difference to the lives of many, many people, and healthcare is certainly a profession that is meaningful, worthwhile and valued by patients.

It is important that medical professionals in all specialisations are academically able to cope with the training, willing to work with people who are ill and therefore vulnerable, have good communication skills and can cope well in sometimes stressful situations. Being dynamic and flexible are also important in a world that is constantly being updated and modernised so that the health professions can deliver even better care tomorrow than today. Every health professional must aim to deliver the best standard of care at all times and have the passion to make a positive difference to people's lives.

Entry routes into the various health professions vary according to the profession, the entry level at which you wish to begin your chosen career, and, sometimes, the institution offering the training course. Therefore, it is important to check the entry route into the profession you're interested in before going too far in making decisions about the future.

When they consider your application, employers and university admissions tutors are looking for evidence of skills, attributes, abilities and qualities that make you an ideal person to become your chosen health professional. They also want to see evidence that you have initiative, integrity and a genuine interest in the profession. This is where suitable work experience is crucial. Undertaking this will allow you to demonstrate that you have an insight into your chosen profession and have learned important skills through the work that you have done; these skills can also be gained through activities such as volunteering, paid work, extracurricular activities and hobbies.

Anyone is eligible to become a health professional if they meet the entry requirements of the training course. The most important of these is probably the academic ability and qualifications required, but these also vary according to the course, the entry level at which you wish to begin your chosen career, and the institution. Health professionals have a range of qualifications, from NVQs and GCSEs to A levels, BScs and even PhDs. There are also different training routes into different avenues of healthcare, and some entry routes even offer monetary supplements or pay in full for you to train. Whatever the entry criteria, there are always ways to progress up the career ladder and starting training is just the beginning of a very long and diverse career that you could, if you choose, follow for the rest of your working life.

Dentist

What does a dentist do?

Dentists are skilled professionals who diagnose and treat problems that affect the teeth, mouth and gums. Dentists work with patients and the general public in a number of ways, preventing and treating dental and oral disease, correcting dental irregularities (particularly in children) and treating dental and facial injuries.

Most dentists work in a practice. These can be large, with many dentists and dental nurses/hygienists; others are small, sometimes with only one dentist. They grow to meet the needs of the local community they support. Dentists often build long-term relationships with patients, caring for people's teeth over many years.

Some dentists are hospital based. They tend to be specialists and see patients who have already been diagnosed with a dental problem. Local dentists pass patients to these specialists from time to time. Hospital dentists also work in emergency situations (e.g. repairing teeth after an accident) or as part of a team working on facial reconstruction as part of emergency care or as a result of elective plastic surgery.

Other dentists practise as community dentists, caring for patients with special needs, including elderly and housebound people and patients with mental or physical disabilities.

Key skills required

- A sound understanding of science: A2 passes in chemistry and one other science.
- Genuine interest in the profession (this can be demonstrated by organising work experience at your local dentist).
- Ability to concentrate for long periods of time.
- Good eyesight and hand–eye co-ordination.
- Good communication skills and empathy.
- Sound organisational skills.
- Business acumen.

Entry routes

In order to practise as a dentist you must first be admitted to one of the UK's 16 dental schools, all of which are attached to universities. Training lasts for five years (six if you enter on the Foundation programme) and competition for entry is high. Direct entry to dental school requires good passes at A2 (or the equivalent) in chemistry and often biology. If you do not have these subjects but have a sound science GCSE profile you could apply for a Foundation course. This will give you an introductory 30-week course covering chemistry, physics and biology.

The British Dental Association has an excellent website that promotes dentistry as a profession and shows that dental schools are open to all candidates who are academically able enough to succeed. Indeed, they are actively working to improve the number of applicants from under-represented groups. If you have the ambition and talent, go for it!

DENTAL SCHOOLS IN THE UK

- Barts and the London School of Dentistry
- Birmingham
- Bristol
- Cardiff
- Dundee
- Edinburgh
- Glasgow
- King's College London
- Leeds
- Liverpool
- Manchester
- Newcastle
- Peninsula College of Medicine and Dentistry
- Queen's University of Belfast
- Sheffield
- University College London

Applicants are expected to take the UKCAT aptitude test (go to www.ukcat. co.uk for more details) and should have a grade A in both A2 chemistry and biology.

Job prospects

There are over 35,000 dentists working in the UK. Most are in private practice, but others work in schools, hospitals and even prisons. There are also opportunities to work in the armed forces, where dentists treat servicemen and women and their family members.

The number of dentists has grown over the past decade. There are also more dental graduates, which has led to greater competition. However, there is still a shortage of NHS dentists in many places, mainly rural areas.

Salary

The starting salary of a newly qualified graduate will depend on where you work. However, as a general rule of thumb a dentist could expect to earn in the region of £28,000 in their first year. This will rise as you grow in experience. A senior dentist in a busy practice could earn in the region of £120,000 and consultant dentists in large hospitals earn in excess of £150,000.

Further information

- British Dental Association, 64 Wimpole Street, London W1G 8YS. Tel: 020 7935 0875. Website: www.bda.org
- NHS jobs: www.jobs.nhs.uk
- *Careers in Dental Care*, NHS Careers
- *Careers in Dentistry*, British Dental Association
- *Getting into Dental School*, Trotman Publishing

Doctor

What does a doctor do?

A doctor is a health professional to whom people turn for help when they have something wrong with their physical or mental health. The doctor is responsible for diagnosing the problem and, if necessary, prescribing a course of treatment. Doctors are also considered 'pillars of the community' and occupy a privileged position in that people allow them into their lives in order to try to make a positive difference to their long-term health. They also work to prevent illness through implementing health promotion initiatives and promoting patient education.

Broadly speaking, doctors employed by the NHS work in either primary care or secondary care. In primary care, patients seek help for a health problem, typically from a general practitioner, or GP. GPs diagnose and treat most conditions in the community setting. In secondary care, patients are referred for further investigation or more specialist care. This may be either as an in-patient, where a patient is admitted to hospital, or as an outpatient, where a patient attends a clinic or regular treatment appointment. In the UK, patients can only access secondary care through their primary care provider.

However, there are opportunities to practise medicine in environments other than the NHS. Examples include working as a doctor on a cruise ship, in the armed forces, in a prison or for immigration services; becoming a medical journalist; or even working abroad, either as a doctor in a hospital or GP practice, or as a volunteer with some of the charitable organisations that work in deprived areas.

Doctors can choose to specialise in a particular aspect of medicine. Doctors working in primary care specialise in being generalists – that is, they know how to manage many different conditions, but there is a limit to the depth of their knowledge and ability to diagnose and treat certain conditions. This is when they refer a patient to a specialist doctor in the secondary care setting. Doctors in this secondary care setting can be further subcategorised, as follows.

- **Physicians** treat conditions, which may be rare or complex, by medication. Physicians either specialise in the types of patient they see, for example paediatricians (children's doctors), or elderly care physicians, or according to a different region in the body, for example cardiologists (heart and circulation), neurologists (the nervous system) or ophthalmologists (eyes).

- **Surgeons** treat conditions by performing surgery. Surgeons can specialise in the conditions or patients they treat, for example orthopaedics (the skeleton), paediatrics (children's surgeon) or trauma (patients who have suffered accidents) but some surgeons work as general surgeons. General surgeons perform many routine operations and often work in the accident and emergency ward of a hospital.

- **Diagnosticians** specialise in performing investigations to diagnose and treat patients. Examples include radiologists (doctors who specialise in interpreting clinical imaging or perform medical procedures under imaging guidance) and pathologists (doctors who diagnose conditions from samples of tissues, fluid, etc. taken from the body).

Deciding to become a doctor opens up a world of opportunities, whether it is working with different types of people, specialising in diagnosing and managing various different health problems, or applying various skills to a multitude of different situations. Whatever type of doctor you choose to become, you will receive a great deal of training and gain much experience to enable you to become an expert in your chosen field.

Becoming a doctor isn't an easy option – it takes years of study, determination and hard work. However, it is a very rewarding career and one that will be stimulating, diverse and fulfilling every day. No two patients are the same, so it is important to have many different skills to be able to cope with the demands of the job: some of these are highlighted below.

Diagnosing and treatment planning form the basis of the majority of doctors' workloads, so it is important for any doctor to have good problem-solving skills and be able to acquire, assess, apply and integrate new knowledge to deliver the best care possible. Some aspects of diagnosis and the treatment plan involve listening to patients and their families, particularly their concerns and expectations, so being able to listen whilst showing respect, being polite and courteous, and not being judgmental, are important too.

DISPELLING MYTHS ABOUT MEDICINE

Medical schools were traditionally overwhelmingly populated by white, male middle- and upper-class students, often educated at independent schools and sometimes with parents who were doctors. However, over the last 30 years, there have been considerable efforts to make medical

(Continued on the following page)

schools more representative of the communities they serve. This has led to significant increases in the number of women, mature students, individuals with disabilities, people from ethnic and cultural minorities and people from all social classes entering the world of medicine. In particular, the graduate entry routes and the modified medicine courses for students who have attended an underperforming school are initiatives that have proved very successful and have paved the way for widening access to medical school.

Making medicine more accessible for all means that the best possible care is provided for all patients and the most suitable people become doctors. There should be no stereotypes as to who is or who is not suited to study medicine. Medicine is accessible to all students, regardless of background. If you have the academic potential and the desire to go into medicine you should go for it.

Key skills required

Good communication skills are central to being a good doctor. You might be talking to a patient to help them understand their illness at one moment, then talking to a family to help them come to terms with a loved one's illness at the next. As a doctor you will come into contact with many different people on a regular basis and it is important to communicate effectively, efficiently and at the right level for each individual.

In addition, it is important to be honest, open and trustworthy. Patients and colleagues place a great deal of trust in doctors and many of the cases that doctors come across are very personal and embarrassing for patients, so confidentiality and discretion are paramount.

Doctors also need to be good leaders. Patient care is often driven by a doctor, so leadership skills are essential. However, it is not always the case that doctors should always be in charge, particularly if a patient's needs are better dealt with by another health professional, so in such instances it is important that doctors work as part of a team.

They also need to be calm in a crisis, numerate, of above average intelligence, with a passion for science, willing to work long hours and happy to continue to train throughout their long career.

Entry routes

To become a doctor, you must first be trained at medical school. However, getting into medical school is not easy: it is a lengthy and sometimes stressful process that requires determination, optimism and patience. The most important, specific entry requirements are stipulated by each medical school, and most of these relate to qualifications.

GCSEs are important: a minimum of a B (or a C at very few medical schools) in English and maths and a good range of other subjects are needed. Some medical schools even state the number of A*s needed (Birmingham require seven A*s!), although such high requirements are rare. It is best to concentrate on performing to the best of your ability at GCSE with the aim of getting the highest marks possible. This will stand you in good stead for performing well at A level and showing medical schools you have what it takes to study there.

At A level, AAA or A*AB is now necessary for most medical schools, although there are still a few who accept AAB. Not only are grades specified but the subjects studied are also defined – chemistry to A2 is needed for most medical schools, plus another science, typically biology. The third option is up to you. One medical school says that they prefer you to have a third science, but the vast majority actually prefer a third subject that contrasts with the science subjects, just to show that there is some diversity in your academic background. The best thing to recommend is doing your third A level in a subject that you are most likely to get at least an A in, just so you won't be prevented from applying to medical school simply because your grades are not good enough.

Other qualifications that are acceptable include an honours degree in a biology- or chemistry-related field with at least 2:1. If you have a degree in a non-science subject, it may be appropriate to do a one-year access course before applying to medical school; this will provide the foundations for learning about the sciences underlying the study of medicine. Such courses are welcomed by medical schools, and some institutions offering access courses are even linked to specific medical schools (e.g. Brighton and Sussex Medical School with Sussex Downs College). Such links provide more chances to study medicine, for example by offering two opportunities at interview rather than the normal one for all other candidates.

To show your understanding and interest of the medical world, it is important to undertake work experience. This should be somewhere that care is being delivered, for example a hospital, hospice, care home, pharmacy or disabled children's centre. You also need to show that you have a wide range of skills, and you can demonstrate that you have these skills by doing any volunteer work, having a job, taking up positions of responsibility, gaining awards and achievements, and even having a hobby. Try to think outside the box and show that you really know what it takes to be a medical student and/or doctor before you apply. For example, you could even try to spend some time with a funeral director – this will get you used to seeing dead bodies, which will help prepare you for when you have to examine them at medical school (if you apply to a medical school that includes dissection in their curriculum), but also for working as a doctor: death is something you have to be able to deal with in any area of medicine.

As part of the application process, most medical schools require you to sit a UK Clinical Aptitude Test (UKCAT). Some medical schools also ask you to undertake a BioMedical Admissions Test (BMAT). Graduates applying to certain UK medical schools will have to do the Graduate Australian Medical School Admissions Test (GAMSAT).

Medical schools in the UK

There are 31 medical schools in the UK, each differing slightly in what they have to offer and the way they approach medical training. Some medical schools have only around a hundred students; others have well over three hundred in just one year group – so choosing the right social environment for you is important to maximise your learning.

Studying at medical school normally takes five years. The early years are usually based mainly at university, going to lectures and other similar teaching scenarios, with some clinical contact time. As the course progresses, much more teaching is done 'on the job' through frequent, and eventually daily, placements in a clinical setting.

However, in the past few years, some medical schools have changed the duration of the courses they offer according to the people they are trying to attract. One scheme that aims to increase applications from non-traditional applicants is a six-year course for students who are academically able but come from schools that are below average in the quality of teaching they provide. These courses, which are offered by King's College London and Southampton among others, aim to get students up to a certain level before integrating them with students studying the five-year course later on in the degree.

It is also worth pointing out that some medical schools, such as St George's, University of London, and the University of East Anglia, offer a reduced grade requirement for students from underperforming schools for the traditional five-year course. This means that medical school can be an achievable goal for students who have been less fortunate than most in the place where they have studied for their A levels.

Training and development

Graduating from medical school is just the start of a fulfilling, challenging and worthwhile career that requires lifelong learning and dedication to ensure the best possible care is delivered for all patients.

After medical school come the Foundation training years – Foundation Year 1 (also known as F1 or FY1) and Foundation Year 2 (F2 or FY2). These two years are the junior doctor years, when doctors are practising medicine, learning on the job, and making a real difference to people's lives, but still have some way to go before being allowed to practise some of the more sophisticated and difficult aspects of medicine. During these two years, junior doctors rotate through a series of different specialities, each lasting four months. These specialities are chosen by the F1 and F2 doctors themselves according to what the hospital they are working in has to offer. This allows them to tailor their learning to the areas they are most interested in and to develop a good knowledge base that will be beneficial for their chosen speciality.

After F1, doctors register with the General Medical Council (GMC) before commencing their F2. This is rather like getting a provisional driving licence before gaining a full licence after proving you're able to drive.

After F2 comes either the speciality training or GP training. This is when doctors decide on the area they wish to specialise in and work mainly in this field to gain more experience of the typical conditions and diseases that form the basis of the speciality.

Speciality training (ST) ranges in duration from three years to eight years, depending on the speciality. During this time, doctors are given greater responsibilities for caring for patients and working in the hospital, for example running clinics on their own or performing operations as the main surgeon. After successfully completing speciality training, the doctor will then be a consultant.

From 2011, **GP training** will take five years to complete. It involves rotating through various hospital specialities that deal with conditions or types of patient commonly seen in general practice. This can include specialities such as paediatrics, obstetrics and gynaecology, and psychiatry. The final part of GP training involves working in a general practice to learn on the job before becoming a fully fledged GP.

Job prospects

Job prospects are good after you have completed your training: there are opportunities in a wide range of different disciplines. However, you are promoted on the basis of your competence so it is vital that you continue to learn and train even if you become an established consultant. Top jobs are very hard to get and only go to the most dedicated and skilled practitioners.

Salary and other benefits

One of the rewards of being a doctor is the income. Doctors are assigned a basic salary plus a supplement, which can be up to 50% of the basic salary and is dependent on the number of hours worked and the intensity of the workload. So, for example, an F1 doctor working in the middle to upper supplement banding (the most common banding option chosen) can expect to earn £33,285 for the year. As the job begins to demand greater responsibility and improved knowledge for each subsequent year of work, salary increases year on year to reflect this. An F2 typically earns £41,285, and doctors in speciality training can expect to earn between £44,117 and £69,369 (including the banding supplement). Once qualified, consultants earn between £74,504 and £176,242, again depending on the work they do and the hours they work.

GPs can earn £53,249 to £80,354 if they are employed by a GP practice (a salaried GP), or from £80,000 to £120,000 if they choose to become self-employed (an independent GP).

It is also important to note that doctors can make the job fit around them rather than the other way around. This means that training can be flexible if requested, and can be done part time. The medical profession appreciates that there is life outside work, so your career can be tailored to reflect this.

Final thoughts

Medicine is a hard profession to break into and can be a very stressful, difficult and, at times, emotionally draining profession to work in.

Deciding to become a doctor is not something that should be considered lightly. Medicine couples science with problem-solving and demands communication skills that are second to none. It also necessitates a great deal of precision, perfection and persistence to ensure that you help every single patient to the highest possible standards. However, medicine is a great career as it is pushes the boundaries of modern technology, it's a job that is completely different every day, and it involves working with other people, whether they are some of the great minds of the medical world or ordinary patients, who often have the most wonderful and inspiring stories to tell.

MEDICAL SCHOOL UNDERGRADUATE PROFILE

My name's Marie Locke and I'm coming towards the end of my fourth year of studying medicine at Brighton and Sussex Medical School. I love the work I do, whether it's talking to patients, helping to make diagnoses, taking blood or even assisting in theatres. However, if you'd have told me six years ago that I would one day become a doctor, I think I would have just laughed and thought you were crazy.

I'm the first person in my family to go to university, so considering a career in medicine – one of the most prestigious and competitive degrees available – was never something that an ordinary 'muggle' like me did. My mother works as a pharmacy technician and my dad works in an office; I can count on one hand the number of GCEs they got between them and neither went on to even do A levels. I'm not saying that my parents are stupid by any means, but becoming an academic was never something that was expected of me and is a world that I have had to learn about with them. My mother, especially, has always supported me in everything that I have done and, even if she couldn't help with my chemistry homework, she tried to make everything in my life as stress-free as possible! This has enabled me to work to my full potential, regardless of my family background or what was expected of me according to my socio-economic

(Continued on the following page)

status. I'm not saying that it's been an easy ride or a simple task to now be studying medicine, but I hope I'm an example of what perseverance and dedication can be rewarded with.

The type of people who become doctors cannot be stereotyped and it is simply a matter of whether a person has the passion to make it that determines whether an individual can become a doctor or not. So, whether you are male or female, old or young, black or white, or rich or poor, the career path you wish to follow is completely up to you and you should let nothing hold you back!

Further information

- BioMedical Admissions Test (BMAT), Cambridge Assessment, 1 Hills Road, Cambridge CB1 2EU. Tel: 0122 355 3366. Website: www. admissionstests.cambridgeassessment.org.uk
- British Medical Association (BMA), BMA House, Tavistock Square, London WC1H 9JP. Tel: 020 7387 4499. Website: www.bma.org.uk
- General Medical Council (GMC), Regent's Place, 350 Euston Road, London NW1 3JN. Tel: 0845 357 8001. Website: www.gmc-uk.org
- Graduate Australian Medical School Admissions Test (GAMSAT). Website: www.gamsatuk.org
- NHS Careers. Tel: 0345 606 0655. Website: www.nhscareers.nhs.uk
- UK Clinical Aptitude Test (UKCAT). Tel: 0161 855 7409. Website: www.ukcat.ac.uk
- *Tomorrow's Doctors*, General Medical Council
- *Becoming a Doctor*, BMA
- *Careers in Medicine*, NHS Careers
- *The Essential Guide to Becoming a Doctor*, Blackwell
- *Getting into Medical School 2012 entry*, Trotman Publishing
- *Medicine Uncovered*, Trotman Publishing
- *Progression to Medicine, Dentistry and Optometry*, UCAS
- *So You Want to be a Brain Surgeon? A Medical Careers Guide*, Ward and Eccles
- *Working in Community Healthcare*, VT Lifeskills

- *Working in Hospitals*, VT Lifeskills
- *British Medical Journal (BMJ)*
- *The Lancet*
- *Student BMJ*

Nurse

What does a nurse do?

Nursing is a unique occupation that offers you the chance to offer care to people when they are vulnerable and in need of support. Recent changes in professional qualifications and expansions in the role of the nurse mean that there has never been a more exciting time to join the nursing profession. Nurses are crucial members of the multi-professional healthcare team; and the number and variety of nursing roles is extensive. Once qualified as a registered nurse you will have the opportunity to work in a range of environments including NHS and independent hospitals, GPs' surgeries, clinics, nursing and residential homes, occupational health services, voluntary organisations, schools, the armed forces and industry. Today there are greater opportunities for nurses to take more responsibility for patient care and to become specialists and advanced practitioners in many areas, for example intensive care, cancer care and mental health.

Key skills

- The desire to help people who are often unable to help themselves.
- The ability to work hard and be able to cope with sometimes stressful conditions.
- The ability to cope with distressing situations and injuries.
- The ability to work in a team.
- Good communication skills.
- A sound understanding of science.
- Numeracy.
- The ability to lead when necessary and take initiative.

Nurses also need to be literate. They must show they can read and understand written English; and they also need to be able to communicate on paper, so many nursing courses expect you to write a brief essay as part of the application process. You also need to demonstrate competency in numeracy, so if you apply to study nursing you will have to undertake a short numeracy test during your interview day.

Entry requirements

If you want to become a nurse, you need to apply for a university degree in nursing. This is what the vast majority of nurses do now – the days of a nursing Diploma are coming to an end. To be successful you need to demonstrate a strong educational profile and a clear commitment to your chosen branch of nursing. Your GCSE profile must include English language, maths and science at grades A–C. Candidates usually require a minimum of 240 UCAS tariff points at A level (typically CCC) or equivalent.

- A/AS levels – your combination must include two A2 grades.
- BTEC National Diploma Health Studies – MMM.
- BTEC Higher Diploma Health Science – Pass.
- Access to Health/Nursing/Science – this should be passed with all core subjects and a minimum of six passes, 33 merits and six distinctions.

All applicants need to demonstrate success at study in the previous three to five years. Although no specific subjects are required, it is useful to study health- or science-related courses. Also, care experience may be beneficial.

When you apply you should expect to be asked about the skills you have and how these might relate to nursing. These skills could include team building, leadership and communication. You should also think about what branch of nursing interests you most, and why. It is also very important to show that you have some meaningful work experience. This does *not* have to be hospital-based. What they are looking for is evidence that you are a 'people person' used to working with people who need care; so you could, for example, work in a hospice as a volunteer, work with children in a school or youth club, take part in charity work that brings you into contact with the public, or work with a homeless charity. Whatever you do, you need to show that you are someone with the caring instincts that all nurses need.

Training and development

Career progression in the NHS is more clear since Agenda for Change was introduced is 2004. The system requires every employee to have a Personal Development Plan (PDP). This will help nurses to become more aware of gaps in their knowledge and competencies, and to identify relevant further training. All learning should be recorded in a portfolio and can include less formal education through in-house training, joining a journal club, reflective practice and studying on interactive learning websites.

For clinically-based nurses the top of the career ladder is the consultant nurse or midwife. Involving specialist practice, leadership, teaching and research, these senior nurses are required to gain a minimum of a Masters level qualification. Non-clinically based nurses can develop their career in management, research or education.

Job prospects

Career prospects depend on job availability throughout the UK. At present this is generally favourable. Once qualified, graduates are equipped to work as a nurse anywhere in the world. The NHS employs around 400,000 qualified nursing staff in England. Other employers include private healthcare organisations, charities and the armed forces.

Following successful completion of your degree and registration with the Nursing and Midwifery Council, you will be able to apply for staff nurse posts in your branch specialism, in the community or in hospitals. New treatments and techniques are introduced all the time so it is essential that nurses update their skills and knowledge on an ongoing basis through continuing professional development (CPD). If you become a nurse and want to progress, you must therefore be willing to continue to study outside your normal working hours.

There are plenty of possibilities for career progression in nursing. With further education, training and experience you can move into nursing and healthcare management, research, education, health promotion and education or nurse consultant roles.

Salary

The current starting salary for a nurse outside London is £21,176. This will rise with time and experience. A senior nurse can expect to be paid a minimum of £30,000, rising to £45,000 for a nurse consultant. This is the top position in the nursing profession. The maximum salary a nurse consultant can earn is £67,000, but this is paid only to the top nurses in the largest hospitals.

Further information

- NHS Careers (www.nhscareers.nhs.uk)
- Royal College of Nursing (www.rcn.org.uk)
- *Careers Uncovered: Nursing and Midwifery*, Trotman Publishing

Physiotherapist

What does a physiotherapist do?

Physiotherapy is the leading therapeutic profession in the NHS. It is an absorbing and fascinating way of working with people in a positive way to improve or maintain their health. Physiotherapists work with patients, mainly through the use of exercise and manual therapies, to help them regain mobility, independence and wellbeing; and they work closely with other professionals.

Degree programmes in physiotherapy provide both university experience and the experience of working with people in healthcare settings. Students go into clinical settings to work with qualified physiotherapists and other health professionals, for example nurses, doctors, and occupational therapists. This balance of academic and work-based learning is excellent preparation for a career in healthcare.

Physiotherapists work with patients of all ages and deal with a range of conditions affecting the soft tissues, joints, bones, nervous system, heart and lungs. They treat joint and spinal problems and help people overcome the effects of falls, sports injuries or other accidents. They also work in health promotion, leading community exercise programmes and back care classes.

They work in a variety of settings, the majority being hospital-based, and see both in-patients and outpatients. In-patient care involves working in intensive care, post-operative care, neurological rehabilitation (for instance helping patients after a stroke or head injury), paediatrics and all other general surgical wards. Outpatient clinics offer support to people who are well enough to cope at home or are recovering from an injury. Physiotherapists also work in the community, visiting patients at home and in palliative contexts.

A minority of physiotherapists work in private practice, which is more lucrative than NHS work.

Key skills

You should:

- be an enthusiastic person with a good academic record
- be prepared to continue to learn and develop new skills
- be well-motivated and happy to work on your own or in a team
- be confident in dealing with a variety of patients
- have good communication skills
- be happy to be 'hands on' with a patient: nearly all the work is physical rather than drug-based therapy, so you need to be willing to have tactile contact with people every day
- have completed suitable work experience placements and show a genuine awareness of the role of physiotherapy – not all physios work in the sports arena!

Entry requirements

To become a practising physiotherapist individuals need to have completed a degree course recognised by the Health Professions Council (HPC). Most of these involve full-time study, but there are also part-time courses.

Most good departments will expect a candidate to have at least one science A level (or equivalent), preferably biology or chemistry. Where two sciences are not offered at A2, another is often required at AS. Entry standards vary, but most departments now make offers of BBB rising to ABB (or equivalent).

The course consists of theory and practice – a large part of the emphasis at the University of Brighton, for example, is on acquiring physiotherapy skills before going on to clinical placements; and the same is true of most other departments in the UK. Teaching consists of tutorials, practicals, seminars, workshops and lectures, according to what most suits the learning material.

Competition for places is keen and it is essential to gain healthcare-related work experience. This may be through a local NHS or private physiotherapy clinic or through voluntary work with a health charity.

Graduates with a first degree in a relevant subject, such as a biological science, psychology or sports science, may be eligible for an approved accelerated two-year degree programme leading to a physiotherapy qualification.

Training involves periods of theory, and clinical experience obtained by working with patients in various healthcare settings. Newly qualified physiotherapists usually spend time in the NHS, working on rotation to gain experience in different settings.

Job prospects

There are over 40,000 chartered physiotherapists working in the UK. Around 60% of them work in the NHS. They are employed by NHS acute and primary care trusts, GP practices and health centres, private practices, residential homes, special schools, sports centres and clinics. One-fifth of physiotherapists are self-employed, dividing their time between work in different settings, or working in private practice.

Salary

Salaries for newly qualified physiotherapists in the NHS start from £21,000 a year. With experience and specialist skills, earnings can rise from around £24,000 to £33,000 a year. Physiotherapists who reach advanced or consultant level may earn £45,000 or more. NHS employees living in and around London are paid extra. Pay varies for physiotherapists who work outside the NHS.

Further information

- Chartered Society of Physiotherapy (CSP), 14 Bedford Row, London WC1R 4ED. Tel: 020 7306 6666. Websites: www.csp.org.uk and www.jobescalator.com
- *Getting into Physiotherapy Courses*, Trotman Publishing
- *Thinking of a Career as a Physiotherapist?*, CSP

CHAPTER 10

LAW

An introduction to law

Law is one of the most popular choices of profession among teenagers. Most people only think of two roles in the legal profession – solicitor and barrister. However, there are other jobs in the legal profession that are worth considering too.

There are three different legal systems in the UK: England and Wales share the same system, while Northern Ireland and Scotland each have their own separate judicial system. A wide range of jobs is available, with solicitors making up the largest occupational group. Solicitors offer advice to clients, who can be both individuals and businesses. The majority of solicitors work in small practices dealing with mostly domestic issues such as buying and selling property, drawing up wills, dealing with minor disputes and working with couples in the process of divorce.

Barristers do not have direct contact with the general public. They are employed by the Crown or by the defendant's solicitor to represent the Crown or the defendant in court. They attempt to persuade a magistrate, jury or judge to accept their case for or against the Crown.

A number of people in legal services are self-employed, including most barristers and many solicitors. Major employers include private legal firms, Her Majesty's Courts Service and the Crown Prosecution Service.

There are over 100,000 practising solicitors in England and Wales, around 17,000 barristers, and many others employed in the legal sector.

Barrister

What does a barrister do?

Barristers are advocates. This means that they represent clients in court. They present the case for the client in the hope that the jury or judge will be persuaded of their case. Barristers are appointed by the Crown to prosecute a case or by the defence to defend a client from the charges put before the court. The time spent in court varies according to the area of law in which the barrister practices. Here is an example of some, but not all, of the areas of law that a barrister might work in.

- **Common and criminal law** is the most well-known area. It involves presenting cases in court. The work is unpredictable and hours can be long. Barristers working in this area need to be confident, articulate and quick-witted as they cross-examine witnesses. Barristers often have to travel to work in courts away from their home or 'chambers'. (A chamber is an office that barristers use to prepare cases.)
- **Chancery** – this work is mostly office-based and deals with disputes regarding trusts, estates and contracts.
- **Employment law** is mainly contract- and statute-based. It may involve up to four days a week in court.
- **Family law** requires a barrister to represent a client in a divorce, child custody case or similar family dispute. The role is often as a mediator – trying to find a solution to a dispute in order to avoid long and expensive legal trials.
- **Personal injury and clinical negligence** – barristers in this area of law are advocates for patients, employees or individuals involved in accidents. An interest in medical matters is helpful.

Whichever type of law they choose, a barrister's work is likely to include:

- taking instruction from solicitors regarding clients
- giving written legal opinions on the likelihood of success in a court case
- conducting research in order to use that research as part of the case for the prosecution or defence
- cross-examining witnesses and presenting a compelling case to a jury or judge
- working with organisations such as accountants, the police and architects for the benefit of the client.

Most barristers are self-employed. The hours they work can be long and involve evening preparation and travel. Most barristers work in offices called chambers. They may have their own office or share one with other barristers.

Some work in government departments and agencies such as the Crown Prosecution Service and the Government Legal Service. These barristers are often referred to as prosecution barristers as they present cases on behalf of the crown.

Key skills required

You should:

- have a level of academic ability that will enable you to cope with complex legal documents and points of law
- be confident, articulate and able to think on your feet in debate
- be happy to work long hours, in sometimes stressful situations, and travel too to find work
- be discreet and honest
- have a good eye for detail and enjoy reading, writing and research
- be able to avoid becoming emotionally involved in distressing cases – you may have to defend a person charged with rape or child abuse, or be involved in a stressful child custody case
- have good social skills – you will meet people from all walks of life.

Entry routes

The two main stages to qualifying as a barrister are the academic stage and the vocational stage.

At the academic stage, candidates need to obtain a good honours degree, which in practice usually means at least a 2:1. If the applicant has a law degree they will need to complete the Bar Vocational Course (BVC), a one-year full-time course taken at a college of law.

If the applicant does not have a law degree, they need to take the conversion course, which is a one-year full-time course taken at a college of law. This is called the Graduate Diploma in Law (GDL) and is an intensive law training programme that attempts to distil the main elements of a law degree into 12 months. It is full time and very intense. After completing that course, you would take the Bar Vocational Course.

The Bar Vocational Course (BVC) is practical and includes interviewing, report writing, case preparation and negotiation as well as legal knowledge.

There are eight institutions across England and Wales offering the BVC.

In order to study for the BVC a trainee has to become a member of one of the Inns of Court. All four Inns are in London and arrangements are made for those studying in other areas.

After the BVC, the final stage of training is pupillage, a year spent working and training with an experienced barrister. Trainees spend time shadowing and observing their pupil supervisor, gradually taking on cases as they gain experience.

Training to become a barrister is a very competitive and often costly process. You need to pay for your GDL or BVC course, which will cost several thousand pounds, and there are no automatic grants to help you to pay. Unlike trainee solicitors, whose firms pay this fee, it is rare that trainee barristers will find a sponsor. That being said, there are grants and bursaries available, as well as Career Development Loans. Full details can be found at the College of Law website.

Becoming a barrister is very competitive. At each stage it is very important that applicants show their commitment to the profession and that they have some knowledge of what the work entails. It can be possible to apply for periods of work experience (known as mini-pupillages) at barristers' chambers. Again this is very competitive.

At each stage there are more applicants than places. Once you have qualified, it may be hard to secure a permanent place (known as a tenancy) in a set of chambers. Remember that you are essentially self-employed.

Barristers have to keep up to date by undertaking continuing professional development (CPD) each year.

Job prospects

There are more than 12,000 practising self-employed barristers. Around 3,000 barristers work as salaried employees for large organisations such as specialist commercial law firms and investment or finance companies, and around 1,300 work in government bodies including the Crown Prosecution Service and the Government Legal Service.

Vacancies for barristers may be advertised in specialist publications such as *The Barrister* and *The Lawyer*.

Salary

Unlike trainee solicitors who join a firm as an employee, barristers are self-employed. As a result, a starting salary for a barrister who is training (in pupillage) can be as low as £10,000. Once qualified, the earnings will depend on how well-known you become. The average salary varies, but a CPS barrister can earn between £30,000 and £80,000 per annum. Others can earn a lot more, but they are in the minority.

Further information

- Advocacy Training Council, Treasury Office, Lincoln's Inn, London WC2A 3TL. Website: www.advocacytrainingcouncil.org
- Bar Council, 289–293 High Holborn, London WC1V 7HZ. Tel: 020 7242 0082. Website: www.barcouncil.org.uk
- Bar Standards Board, 289–293 High Holborn, London WC1V 7HZ. Tel: 020 7611 1444. Website: www.barstandards.org.uk
- Crown Prosecution Service (CPS), 50 Ludgate Hill, London EC4M 7EX. Tel: 020 7796 8000. Website: www.cps.gov.uk
- Her Majesty's Courts Service (HMCS), 102 Petty France, London SW1H 9AJ. Tel: 0845 456 8770. Website: www.hmcourts-service.gov.uk
- *Law Uncovered*, Trotman Publishing

Solicitor

What does a solicitor do?

Solicitors give legal advice to their clients and act on their behalf in legal matters. A client might need advice about buying a house, making a will or resolving a dispute. Solicitors also advise couples who are considering a divorce and discussing custody of children.

Clients can also include businesses, voluntary bodies, charities and government departments.

The main responsibilities of a solicitor include:

- advising members of the public or organisations about the law and its impact on them
- working with a barrister to prepare a client's case before it is presented in court
- some solicitors represent clients directly in court (as an advocate), although in practice this is rare in criminal cases
- drafting letters, contracts and other legal documents on behalf of a client, mindful of the law and its impact upon them
- researching reports, legal documents and past cases in order to offer advice to a client or prepare a case for court.

Once they are fully qualified, solicitors tend to specialise in a particular area of work. The main areas are as follows.

- **Corporate law** is devoted to advising and acting on behalf of companies and organisations. Most large city firms have corporate departments whose aim is to prepare legal papers for business clients.
- **Employment law** involves offering legal advice to corporate clients about employment contracts, discrimination and health and safety law.
- **Residential and commercial conveyancing** – the sale and purchase of property or land. This is the area of law that most members of the general public come into contact with. Many small local solicitors' firms devote the lion's share of their business to this form of business, working with individuals and organisations.

- **Litigation** deals with civil disputes.
- **Family law** involves giving advice to individuals and families regarding marriage troubles or issues relating to children. It also deals with issues relating to the beginning or end of a relationship (e.g. marriage, divorce, etc).
- **Wills and probate** – when you die your assets need to be distributed to your family and friends. A will is a means of passing on your wishes in a legally binding form. It is very important to have a will, particularly if you have children. Solicitors advise clients about such matters and help process the estate of a deceased person (probate). They also deal with the affairs of people who die without a will.
- **Central and local government** – acting for the Civil Service and local government departments, employees, ministers and councillors. Many government bodies and large corporate clients employ their own 'in house' legal teams that will include solicitors.
- **Crown Prosecution Service** – this is an organisation that is tasked with the job of deciding whether a case presented by the police should be prosecuted. The CPS is staffed with solicitors who are able to assess the evidence and determine whether a case is likely to succeed.

Key skills required

- A high level of education: you need to be bright to work in the law as the information you read and assess is often intellectually demanding.
- Drive and determination: the law requires you to work hard and show personal initiative at times.
- Enthusiasm: it is vital that your clients feel sure that you can win the case for them and this will come across if you are enthusiastic and positive.
- Attention to detail: it is essential that a solicitor has a keen eye for detail, can spot an error in a document before it is too late and is very well organised. This can be painstaking and time consuming. It is not a profession that suits the disorganised or lazy!
- Curiosity and flexibility: lawyers need to enjoy dealing with new ideas and adapting to new challenges.
- Capacity for hard work: the hours can be long and the work stressful with deadlines to meet. You must be willing to work hard at times to meet the needs of the clients. This is particularly true of the larger law firms, where hours can be painfully long.

- Good presentation: clients expect you to be well dressed, articulate and have sound social skills.
- Honesty and integrity: a lawyer must be seen to be trustworthy and someone who will keep secrets.
- Good communication skills: lawyers spend a good deal of time working with people, sometimes people who are under great stress. It is therefore vital that you are a confident communicator and able to persuade a client to adopt a strategy that they may not initially want to follow.

Entry routes

To be eligible to apply for trainee solicitor posts, candidates need to hold one of the following qualifications:

- a qualifying law degree (listed at www.sra.org.uk)
- a degree in any subject, followed by a one-year full-time (or two-year part-time) course leading to the Graduate Diploma in Law (GDL), or the Common Professional Examination (CPE)
- a Senior Status law degree (two years full time or three years part time; some courses are offered via distance learning).
- Fellowship of the Institute of Legal Executives (ILEX).

Law students are also advised to undertake vacation placements in law firms and to gain as much experience as possible by taking part in extracurricular activities such as interviewing competitions, debating, 'mooting' (dummy trials) or pro bono (voluntary) work.

Studying to become a solicitor is an expensive process and there are no automatic bursaries. That being said, the vast majority of law firms do pay part of all of the cost of the training. You can also get grants or awards from the colleges and apply for a Career Development Loan. Do not be put off by the debt as you will earn good money as a solicitor in the long run.

Training and development

Training as a solicitor involves taking the Legal Practice Course (LPC), which lasts one year full time or two years part time, followed by a two-year training contract with a firm of solicitors or an 'in-house' legal department. Part-time training contracts are available. Interim experience as a paralegal may be helpful.

Some firms offering contracts sponsor trainees to undertake the LPC course. Typically, the training contract includes a series of placements ('seats') in different departments of a firm to experience the variety of work undertaken, and a short Professional Skills Course.

Solicitors must undertake 16 hours' continuing professional development (CPD) per year once qualified.

There are also plenty of opportunities – for commercial solicitors in particular – to work abroad.

RECENT GRADUATE PROFILE

One of the UK's leading law firms is Freshfields, who are a major city law firm based in London and round the world. Freshfields is one of the largest law firms in the world (about 5,000 staff globally). They are based in 16 different jurisdictions worldwide with 27 offices.

Susan Wamanga-Wamai joined Freshfields as a trainee solicitor in August 2008, having spent three weeks with the firm as a vacation visitor (i.e. doing work experience) in 2007. Susan studied law at Leeds University and took the LPC at BPP Law School. She went to school at Mount St Mary's College.

During her training contract, Susan spent time in Freshfields' corporate, banking, and restructuring and insolvency departments and went on secondment to Merrill Lynch, an investment bank, and to the firm's Dubai office.

Susan explains her decision to become a lawyer: 'At school I knew that science subjects were not for me and that I was more suited to an arts-based/humanities degree – put simply, I was more interested in words than in numbers. I found law attractive because, in addition to realising that it underlies everything in our society, I thought that it would actually be interesting to study and would help develop analytical and

(Continued on the following page)

problem-solving skills that would be useful in any future career. I was also attracted by the independent study and research involved in a law degree. As well as having taught classes and lectures, a large part of the degree was independent study, which I thought would give me the ability to reach my own conclusions on various topics.

'While at university, I enjoyed applying the law to practical scenarios, which made me want to practise it as a lawyer. In addition to visiting various websites such as the Law Society, Prospects and lawcareers. net and referring to *The Training Contract and Pupillage Handbook*, the best insight into different law firms was provided by representatives of the firms at presentations and law/career fairs. Speaking to lawyers and hearing directly from them what the job involves, its challenges and rewards, was the best way for me to decide that I was suited to a career as a solicitor and, particularly, a City law firm.

'When I first started my vacation scheme, I'd had an idea that City lawyers might be a bit stuffy or distant. I was quickly proved wrong. Just because you're working at a magic circle firm doesn't mean you have to leave your sense of humour at the door. Working with the right people makes a huge difference – so you do need to make sure that you look at a variety of different firms and environments.'

Job prospects

The recent economic downturn has had a significant impact on the legal profession, particularly those practices which rely heavily on conveyancing. As a result, some firms have introduced pay freezes or have stopped recruiting new trainees. This has made it harder than ever for young lawyers to get a job.

Solicitors are employed throughout the UK by firms ranging in size from one or two partners to large organisations with thousands of employees. The number of solicitors has grown overall in recent years and there are now about 125,000 solicitors practising in England and Wales.

Around 75% of solicitors work in private practice. Entry standards vary but are usually quite high, with vacancies in the large firms being heavily over-subscribed.

Vacancies are advertised in national newspapers, the *Law Society Gazette*, *The Lawyer* and on internet sites such as www.lawcareers.net.

Salary

The amount you earn will depend largely on the size of the firm you work for. The minimum wage recommended for a trainee solicitor is currently around £17,000. However, this can be significantly more in prestigious City firms. Most qualified solicitors in the UK earn between £45,000 and £60,000 per annum. Partners in large firms can earn well over £200,000.

It should be pointed out at this stage that 90% of UK solicitors do not work for large firms. Moreover, competition for entry into a large firm is very intense and academic entry standards are very high indeed. It is a myth that all solicitors are immensely wealthy!

Further information

- Government Legal Service (GLS), Chancery House, 53–64 Chancery Lane, London WC2A 1QS. Tel: 020 7649 6023. Website: www.gls.gov.uk
- Institute of Legal Executives (ILEX), Kempston Manor, Kempston, Bedfordshire MK42 7AB. Tel: 01234 841000. Website: www.ilex.org.uk
- www.lawcareers.net
  Law Society, 113 Chancery Lane, London WC2A 1PL. Tel: 020 7242 1222. Websites: www.lawsociety.org.uk and juniorlawyers.lawsociety.org.uk
- Solicitors Regulation Authority, Ipsley Court, Berrington Close, Redditch B98 0TD. Tel: 0870 606 2555. Website: www.sra.org.uk
- *Becoming a Solicitor*, Law Society
- *Getting into Law*, Trotman Publishing
- *Law Uncovered*, Trotman Publishing
- *Prospects Law*, Graduate Prospects
- *The Training Contract and Pupillage Handbook*, Globe Business Publishing
- *Law Society Gazette*

CHAPTER 11

MARKETING, ADVERTISING AND PR

An introduction to marketing, advertising and public relations

This diverse range of professions all share one common theme. They all aim to influence attitudes and behaviour. They work on behalf of others to promote a brand, person or idea. Most professionals in this line of work are creative, artistic, fashion- and trend-conscious and have an inner confidence that enables their ideas to win contracts in a competitive market. Finally, flair and innovation must be combined with an astute business sense and an eye for detail.

Some entrants to these professions do vocational degrees prior to joining, such as bachelor's degrees in marketing, advertising or media and public relations (PR). Others may have a degree in another discipline and obtain appropriate professional qualifications while working.

The industry can be divided broadly into people who work in house for an organisation, and those who work for an agency, providing specialist services to paying clients. Both areas offer jobs in the following.

- **Brand management**: this team will have an acute awareness of the needs of their brand. There are brands in all industries and in rare cases individual celebrities have or are 'brands': the Beckham brand is promoted and protected by a brand management team in the same way as major corporate brands such as Mars, Apple Mac or Next. People working in brand management undertake research, with the marketing team, into local competition in the market, keep the profile of the brand high in the public arena and promote new products or innovations when required.

- **Brand image**: the public relations (PR) team will be responsible for maintaining the image (or perhaps changing the image) of a brand or person. They liaise with the press and other media, arrange events to promote the customer, ensure advertising meets the public needs of the client and protect the client from unwanted attention.

- **Advertising**: developing concepts, words and artwork; sourcing specialists such as models, actors, photographers and film directors; and booking advertising space in relevant media, such as TV, the internet, or newspapers.
- **Marketing**: this is a diverse area including web design, market research, in-house journalism, designing promotional material, organising conferences, press launches and exhibitions. Marketing people often work closely with the PR, advertising and brand management teams. In smaller companies they are one and the same.

Over 750,000 people work in marketing, advertising, PR and sales. Many of these positions are not managerial and do not require graduate entry. However, most senior practitioners are graduates. Employment is found in a wide range of companies, from small to multinational. Many jobs are found in the public sector, in as diverse a range as the Home Office, county councils' executives, the NHS, schools and trades unions.

Most are office jobs and the majority are located in the major cities, with London attracting the lion's share.

Marketing executive

What does a marketing executive do?

The role of the marketing executive is both to raise awareness of a product and to increase sales of the product. Most marketing teams work very closely with PR and advertising executives and the skills they require are very similar. Marketing executives use a wide range of techniques to achieve their aims, including direct mailings, web marketing, press and TV campaigns, advertising billboards and sometimes direct contact with potential customers at events or during telephone campaigns.

Your role as a graduate entrant will depend on the size and nature of the company you join. However, all companies would expect you to undertake research into the market, study competitors' products and look at ways in which you could extend awareness of the product in the market place. You will show creativity in devising, together with the PR team, new campaigns and strategies that you can pitch to a client; and when you have won a bid, your role will be to manage the campaign from start to finish. Finally, you may become involved in writing press copy, organising events and maintaining customer databases.

Key skills required

- Either a degree with a marketing component or a willingness to undertake professional qualifications while working.
- Creativity.
- Industriousness.
- A confident manner when dealing with people.
- Ability to work in a diverse group.
- Ability to work in a stressful and competitive environment.
- Numeracy, articulacy and good writing skills.
- Liveliness, honesty and a sense of humour.
- An interest in current fashions, whatever form they take.

Entry routes

Graduates are encouraged to apply for jobs in marketing regardless of whether they have a marketing-based degree. That being said, a graduate with a degree in marketing from a good university will, on paper, appear to have an advantage. One way of making yourself attractive would be to try and gain an internship (work experience placement) with a company that has a strong sales and marketing department.

In researching for this book, I looked at a number of firms and they all offer pretty similar programmes. One of these firms is Procter & Gamble, a multinational company with hundreds of high street brands under their control, ranging from hair care products such as Pantene to snack foods such as Pringles. The information about them is useful as a guide to anyone interested in the business, regardless of whether you work for them in the future.

Procter & Gamble, like other leading companies, offer short and one-year internships. These are work experience programmes, which are increasingly common across the professions. They are paid positions and are designed to provide a potential applicant with an insight into the career before they commit full time. Firms such as Procter & Gamble tend to enrol people in the final year of their undergraduate course. An internship in marketing will expose you to many different brands and business situations. Many successful interns come back and work for the firm who offered them the place on a permanent basis after they have finished their degree.

Job prospects

Graduate entrants into this profession have a wide spectrum of interests and expertise. Many large companies have structured graduate entry schemes, some of which are solely marketing orientated. Opportunities exist in a variety of fields covering all industries. Employment prospects are good but competition for places in the top companies remains fierce.

Salary

Entry-level marketing positions for graduates pay on average around £23,000 a year. Experienced executives earn over £30,000 rising to £60,000 plus for top executives. A marketing director of a large company can earn well over £100,000 per annum.

Further information

- *Careers 2011*, Trotman Publishing
- *Careers Uncovered: Marketing*, Trotman Publishing
- *The IDM Marketing Guide* – www.theidm.com
- *Inside Careers Guide to Marketing and Sales* – www.insidecareers.co.uk
- www.targetjobs.co.uk
- *Working in Marketing, Advertising and PR*, VT Lifeskills
- *Brand Republic*, www.brandrepublic.com
- *Campaign*, www.campaignlive.co.uk
- *Marketing Week*, www.marketingweek.co.uk

Public relations

What does someone in PR do?

All major companies, organisations and some well-known individuals employ PR companies to manage their image in the public eye. PR in a 24-hour media world is increasingly vital. Celebrities might employ a well-known publicist such as Max Clifford to manage their media relations; and at the other extreme a major international company might employ a top PR company to present their company in a positive light in the world's media. This is not about marketing their products (this is the role of the marketing team), it is more about protecting and enhancing the reputation of the company or individual. Increasingly, PR encompasses protecting online reputations and promoting corporate and social responsibility (this relates to how an organisation is ethically meeting today's environmental and social challenges).

People who work in PR are sometimes employed as part of an in-house team. Others work for PR companies who specialise in particular types of client or industry.

A PR executive could be involved in planning PR campaigns, writing press releases, briefing journalists, updating internet sites, and preparing speeches and presentations for the client's executives. Others may spend most of their time arranging events such as exhibitions, open days and sponsorship deals. This may involve travel, stress and long, sometimes unsocial, hours. The glamorous 'Ab Fab' idea of PR is often far from the truth! That being said, it can be glamorous too, with press parties and lots of celebrity-spotting opportunities.

The job involves working closely with the marketing and media teams, so an awareness of their role is vital. Competition in the industry is intense, so professionals need to be willing to work hard to get and keep demanding clients. The work is mostly office-based and increasingly the major jobs are found in London and a few other major UK cities.

Key skills required

Public relations officers should:

- be able to work under pressure and sometimes in a demanding, fast-moving environment

- be confident in a crisis – this is when PR is most important. A calm voice in such times is often the difference between triumph and disaster
- be aware of trends and fashions that may impact on the PR of a client
- have strong written and oral communication skills – you will spend many hours briefing journalists, writing press releases, talking to clients and potential customers
- have confidence in their own ability and the power to motivate and persuade others
- be organised, pay attention to detail, be careful time managers and show initiative
- be creative, innovative and understand the full range of media opportunities out there to exploit
- have good research and analytical skills – in order to identify potential PR opportunities
- be good team players, willing to work with a variety of different professions all engaged in the same overall objective – to promote the client.

Entry routes

There is no one route into PR. Due to high competition for jobs, many entrants have a degree and, increasingly, a postgraduate qualification. This could be in PR, but other subjects such as media studies, advertising or marketing and communications, English, sociology, politics, business and journalism are common. Large companies may offer graduate programmes, some specialising entirely in PR.

Degree courses usually last three years; some last four years and include a year's work placement. Postgraduate courses in PR and marketing are also available. Many of the best courses are recognised by the Chartered Institute of Public Relations and the Chartered Institute of Marketing.

The top courses are looking for students who have ambition, academic ability and, preferably, active interest and involvement in communications. Most courses balance academic and practical study and nearly all of them have a work placement programme that enables the student to experience work in an agency while completing their course. This clearly gives you an edge when applying for jobs.

Doing unpaid work experience or an internship is good for networking and may increase your chances of employment. The Chartered Institute of Public Relations (CIPR) and the Public Relations Consultants Association (PRCA) websites give advice on sourcing placements.

Training and development

Entrants will usually develop their skills on the job, shadowing more experienced colleagues. Structured graduate training schemes may be available in large consultancies and employers.

The CIPR offers recognised professional qualifications, short courses and a continuing professional development (CPD) scheme.

- CIPR Advanced Certificate: aimed at people with a few years' PR experience or graduates who haven't studied PR. Applicants should have the CIPR Foundation Award or any UK degree or two years' relevant PR employment with five GCSEs (A*–C), including English.
- CIPR Diploma: for more experienced PR practitioners aiming for strategic management PR positions.

See the CIPR website (www.cipr.co.uk) for entry requirements. Both CIPR courses can be studied online.

The PRCA offers face-to-face and online training for their professional qualifications, including:

- PRCA Foundation Course: aimed at recent entrants or people interested in entering PR
- PRCA Advanced Certificate: designed to help practitioners develop the strategic skills necessary to become highly effective.

The CIPR, PRCA and Chartered Institute of Marketing (CIM) run seminars, short courses and training events that can enhance your knowledge of the industry.

Job prospects

PR is a good employer in the UK, with around 50,000 people employed, mostly in London or large cities. In-house work is most common, with retail, central and local government, political parties, unions and the NHS all major players.

Other people in PR work as consultants who might offer bespoke advice to individuals or be employed to work on specific projects, such as the World Cup 2018 bid or the London 2012 Olympics. These jobs can be well paid but they are often freelance, so the risk of unemployment is higher.

Vacancies are advertised by university careers services and recruitment agencies, in national newspapers and specialist publications including *Press Gazette*, *Profile* and *PR Week*. CIPR has a PR jobshop (www.ciprjobs.co.uk) and also publishes lists of voluntary charity-based placements and salaried graduate training schemes.

The *PRCA Yearbook* and Hollis UK *Public Relations Annual* offer useful contact information for networking and speculative applications. See the PRCA website and their jobs board (www.prcajobs.org.uk) for details.

Salary

A new graduate in a reasonable firm might start on between £16,000 and £22,000 a year. Once you are established, the salaries are good without being fantastic. In-house executives will earn £35,000–40,000 per annum. Senior executives and those working for major companies could earn in excess of £100,000 per annum.

Salaries vary widely between industry sectors. Financial, healthcare and business-to-business technology organisations usually pay more.

Further information

- Chartered Institute of Marketing (CIM), Moor Hall, Cookham, Maidenhead, Berkshire SL6 9QH. Tel: 01628 427120. Websites: www.cim.co.uk and www.getin2marketing.com
- Chartered Institute of Public Relations (CIPR), 52–53 Russell Square, London WC1B 4HP. Tel: 020 7631 6900. Website: www.cipr.co.uk
- Public Relations Consultants Association (PRCA), Willow House, 17–23 Willow Place, London SW1P 1JH. Tel: 020 7233 6026. Website: www.prca.org.uk
- *Brand Republic,* www.brandrepublic.com
- www.guardian.co.uk/media

CHAPTER 12

MEDIA

An introduction to professions in the media

The UK has one of the oldest and most established media networks in the world. It is the home of some of the world's oldest and most prestigious newspapers, magazines and journals – the print media. Journalists working in this branch of the profession will write for these titles either as full-time employees or freelance writers.

The UK also has the oldest national television network in Europe. The BBC employs thousands of men and women who work in all aspects of broadcast media, including television, radio and, increasingly, internet-based broadcast journalism. They of course now compete not only with the free-to-air broadcasters such as Channel 4 or ITV, but also with a huge number of satellite channels dominated by Sky.

Finally, the UK is at the cutting edge of independent production, with new and creative companies producing programmes to be broadcast on television or radio. When you add to this the growing demand for web-based media sites, it is no wonder that this profession is growing year on year.

It is a buoyant and dynamic environment to work in, with creative and often young people dominating the agenda. However, securing a job in the media is an ambition shared by a significant number of young people, resulting in a crowded and competitive arena, where opportunities to find work seem increasingly scarce. This fierce market can lead many graduates to feel disillusioned and to some it seems that success has more to do with luck than anything else. The good news is this profession is truly blind to your background or ethnicity. If you are good, persevere and have the courage of your own convictions, you will succeed.

One of the keys to success is to have a clear idea of the demands of the profession, what they look for in new entrants (i.e. the skills that you need to have before you apply) and the willingness to accept lots of rejections before getting the job you crave.

Many young people say they want to work in the media without having a clear idea of exactly what they want to do. This leaves the impression that they lack commitment and focus. For instance, if you have a burning desire to become a print journalist, you need to start writing! Write for school magazines (if you don't have a school magazine, invent it), local newspapers or blogs; or simply create a portfolio of work – it may not have been published, but it will show what you are made of.

What you cannot afford to do is apply without first doing the research and trying to secure some relevant work experience. This will almost certainly be unpaid but it is the foot in the door that helps you on your way. One leading BBC TV presenter I interviewed when writing this book got his first break when he was making tea in a café in Russia that was used by television crews. On the day that the former President of the USSR Mikhail Gorbachev was a victim of an attempted coup, my interviewee was one of the few people present who could speak fluent Russian and English. He joined the BBC crew at the heart of the action and they were impressed enough to offer him a job. Twenty years later, he is a leading BBC correspondent and has spent time in London, Paris, Russia and now the USA.

Students who want to work in TV or radio need to familiarise themselves with the output of the various channels and production companies and ensure that they can comment on this at interview. Likewise, those interested in print journalism should be prepared to offer opinions and ideas on a range of local and national newspapers.

'It can frankly be amazing, the number of people who arrive asking for a job or work experience who do not really understand the business we are in. They just assume that all television companies are the same – they are not! This is lazy and shows me that they are not really serious. You must do your research, be willing to discuss the programmes produced by the company and even suggest new ones! We look for sparky, creative people who know the business and know too its pitfalls!'

(Producer, Channel 4)

Due to space constraints this chapter will focus on only two aspects of the media – print journalism and broadcast journalism. One very useful resource if you are interested in any branch of the media is *Contacts*, a book published annually by Spotlight (www.spotlight.com). It includes details of UK film, radio, television and video production companies, theatre companies, publicity and press representatives and many other media-related organisations. If you're interested in a job in the media it is well worth getting a copy or borrowing it from a library.

Print journalist

What does a print journalist do?

A journalist is employed to find stories of interest and to report them, mostly in print form, in a way that is interesting, succinct and written in a style suitable for their audience. For instance, the readership of the *Financial Times* is very different from that of the *Sun* or *Hello!* magazine. Increasingly print journalists are also involved in the online world, be it with online articles, videos or blogs.

There are thought to be up to 80,000 journalists in the UK, and there are opportunities all over the country, with a concentration of news organisations in major cities.

Journalists often work to strict deadlines and therefore need to be good writers who can work quickly and when under pressure. Journalism is also good fun, for lots of reasons: it is about being there – being outside No. 10 for Barack Obama's visit, at Wembley for the cup final, or maybe reporting at the centre of a natural disaster. The role is about finding out something that no one else knows, and then telling them (always a fun thing to do). You are carefully crafting stories and showing them to other people whether they are in a blog, a glossy magazine or an online video. Journalism is always new and different: you're looking at the event that has just happened, the story that makes today different from yesterday. No two days are the same for a journalist, and this makes for an exciting life. You might even change the world for the better, by bringing important information to the public, for example about a miscarriage of justice.

Journalists do a huge range of different jobs, including reporting, editing copy, writing columns, taking photos, designing for print or web and putting together broadcast packages for internet sites and/or for radio and TV – so don't think that every journalist is like Jeremy Paxman. Many people think that to be a journalist you need to be an aggressive foot-in-the-door reporter. This is not true. Journalists very rarely operate like that, and in most cases it would be counter-productive if they did. Getting a good story depends far more on building a rapport with your contacts and getting them on your side.

A good journalist needs to be inquisitive, interested in people and in what is going on, keen to look into why something has happened, and what its implications are. They need to have ideas, to be able to think creatively, but also to be a good listener.

The vast majority of journalists start out as general news reporters. They are assigned jobs by their news editor and often go out to jobs with a photographer. Most start in small local newspapers, and only the best rise to the challenge of writing for nationals like the *Daily Telegraph* or the *Guardian*. Other types of journalist include sub-editors, who check and shape the reporters' work and add headlines; feature writers, who produce longer pieces that are less time sensitive; and columnists and commentators. Journalists can also specialise in a particular field, e.g. sports, politics or health.

Key skills

You must:

- be a good writer with a sound grasp of the basics of written English – you need not be the best speller in the world, but you do need to know how to write
- be naturally inquisitive – interested in people and events – and have an 'eye' for a good story
- have good communication and people skills
- have an awareness of why something has happened, and what its implications are
- be creative and have ideas
- be a good listener
- pay attention to detail
- be able to win the confidence of all kinds of people
- have a passion for current affairs
- be willing to work hard, often at unsociable times
- be persistent.

Entry routes

A degree in any subject is considered relevant. It is not essential to have a degree in journalism, although a course that offers practical experience in the industry may be useful.

One well-known and respected journalism course is the one offered by City University London. There are others and the broad content of all courses is similar. The information here is specific to City, but it could equally apply to all other institutions. Some courses, including the City University course, are accredited and listed by the National Council for the Training of Journalists (NCTJ), the Periodicals Training Council (PTC) and the Broadcast Journalism Training Council (BJTC).

In humanities subjects, the teaching at university level would consist of a lecture and perhaps a seminar, with the bulk of the student's time being spent in the library, reading, taking notes, and writing essays and presentations. A journalism degree is also likely to include some lectures, perhaps about current affairs or media law. On a practical journalism degree, much of the teaching is likely to be in smaller groups. Students will carry out research and interviews to create news stories and features for websites or newspaper pages, and/or to produce broadcast packages. All this will be done under the guidance of tutors.

If you are looking at journalism courses, check how much of this kind of work is offered in any course you are interested in. Doing this kind of practical work is the only way to learn enough to get a job as a professional journalist. The theory might be fine up to a point, but there is no substitute for completing journalistic tasks to a deadline. Good journalism courses focus on being in the right place at the right time, getting the important information, and doing some work to a deadline. Check that the course you are thinking about has just such extensive hands-on journalistic work, with input and guidance from tutors.

Any journalism course leader will also expect students to do some extra journalism in their spare time. This might include working on a student newspaper, and is almost certain to include professional work placements as well. Tutors might help with getting placements in the early stages, although employers in journalism value students who have the determination to get their own placements. Be prepared to take on unpaid journalism work, as it is rare to get a paid job in journalism without having done around four or five months' work experience.

Training and development

If you graduate with an accredited journalism degree you will start work and all additional training will be carried out on the job. If not, you might be wise to undertake a postgraduate journalism qualification. Details can be found at the end of the chapter.

On a local newspaper, trainees are normally appointed on a two-year contract, with a probationary period of three to six months. Trainees without a pre-entry qualification may be expected to study on day release for NCTJ exams, including shorthand and law.

Some big news groups, including the BBC and Trinity Mirror, run in-house training schemes. Some national newspapers also have similar schemes. Competition for places is fierce.

A variety of training providers, including the National Union of Journalists (NUJ), offer short courses to help journalists learn new skills and adapt to changing technologies.

Salary

New journalists in a local news organisation may start on around £12,000.

With experience, senior reporters can earn around £22,000. The top journalists in national news operations can earn £80,000 or more.

Further information

- National Council for the Training of Journalists (NCTJ), The New Granary, Station Road, Newport, Saffron Walden, Essex CB11 3PL. Tel: 01799 544014. Website: www.nctj.com
- *In Print: The Guardian Guide to a Career in Journalism*, Guardian Books
- *Careers Uncovered: Journalism*, Trotman Publishing
- *Careers 2011*, Trotman Publishing

Broadcast journalist

What does a broadcast journalist do?

The primary difference between a broadcast and a print journalist is that a broadcast journalist's news items are presented on television, radio or online rather than in printed form. Broadcast journalists do broadly the same thing as print journalists, with the emphasis being on how the story will 'look' on the TV and sound like on the radio. Broadcast journalists most often combine their journalistic role with presenting, perhaps as a newsroom anchor, presenting the news on the BBC, Sky or ITV. They might become a special correspondent, reporting on a wide range of matters from foreign affairs to education. These broadcasters are often specialists with a particular academic background that assists them in their job. A BBC economics correspondent, for example, will usually have a first degree in economics or finance. That is not always the case, particularly when a broadcaster becomes a well-known interviewer such as a Jeremy Paxman or a John Humphrys.

Whether they present or not, most also carry out a normal journalistic role, writing scripts, preparing for interviews and working in the cutting room doing voice overs for pictures. As such they work closely with programme producers and editors.

Radio journalists often record and edit their own material, using specialised equipment. In television, reporters are traditionally accompanied by a camera operator and sometimes sound and lighting technicians. Increasingly, however, they are expected to capture video material themselves.

Key skills required

Research I carried out with Channel 4 and the Broadcast Journalism Training Council suggests the following skills are essential:

- verbal reasoning
- interviewing
- listening
- writing.

Most good journalists:

- have a curious and inquisitive mind
- have a good general knowledge
- are empathetic, patient and understand what will make a good news story.

You have to meet deadlines: this means that you will often have to work quickly and under pressure. You need to be able to express, analyse and condense information, be resourceful, persistent, truthful and accurate. Understanding historical context can be very important for some jobs.

Those who present the news need additional skills, including:

- a good voice
- the ability to speak clearly and naturally
- the ability to master the skill of telling a story.

It is also worth remembering that presenters are simply the top of a very large, wide-based production pyramid and all the people in that pyramid are crucial to getting a bulletin or programme on air. All these people need to have essential broadcast journalism knowledge and skills.

Entry routes

The route is similar to print journalism, although the employers and the postgraduate qualifications are different. The main employers in the UK are the BBC, ITN, Sky and Channel 4. There are also many new commercial broadcasters out there.

The expansion of satellite television, 24-hour rolling news and digital radio mean that there are now many more jobs out there, but the competition remains fierce. It is essential to gain extensive work experience, for example in student, hospital or community media. Many journalists work freelance or on fixed-term contracts.

The large majority of broadcast journalists have a degree. This may be in any subject or one that is linked to journalism.

There are three main entry routes into broadcast journalism:

- **The pre-entry route**: entrants join a broadcast organisation after completing a degree or postgraduate course in broadcast journalism. Most courses last one academic year and are accredited by the BJTC.
- **The direct entry route**: new entrants are recruited into an employer's training scheme, for example with the BBC or Sky, direct from university. Competition for such places is fierce. It is important to check entry requirements with the employer.
- **The sideways route**: some people move into radio or television after gaining experience in newspapers.

Entry requirements for pre-entry journalism courses vary: you should check with course providers for specific details. The BJTC website offers advice on how to assess courses.

Training and development

Employers may offer technical training in the use of recording and editing equipment. Short courses in specific journalistic skills or new technologies are run by organisations such as BBC Training and Development, BJTC, NUJ and NCTJ. Colleges and private training providers also offer short courses.

Salary

Salaries for trainees and new entrants start from around £16,000 a year.

Salaries for more experienced broadcast journalists may range from £27,000 to £40,000 per year. Some senior broadcast journalists, such as Paxman, can earn more than £100,000 a year.

Freelance rates vary, depending on experience and track record. The National Union of Journalists (NUJ) and the Broadcasting Entertainment Cinematograph and Theatre Union (BECTU) can advise on rates. Broadcast journalists may receive allowances for working shifts and unsocial hours.

Further information

- BBC Recruitment, PO Box 48305, London W12 6YE. Tel: 0870 333 1330. Website: www.bbc.co.uk/jobs
- Broadcast Journalism Training Council (BJTC), 18 Miller's Close, Rippingale near Bourne, Lincolnshire PE10 0TH. Tel: 01778 440025. Website: www.bjtc.org.uk
- National Council for the Training of Journalists (NCTJ), The New Granary, Station Road, Newport, Saffron Walden CB11 3PL. Tel: 01799 544014. Website: www.nctj.com
- Radio Academy, 5 Market Place, London W1W 8AE. Tel: 020 7927 9920. Website: www.radioacademy.org
- *The Broadcast Journalism Handbook*, Pearson Education
- Full details of all good undergraduate and postgraduate journalism courses can be found on this excellent website: www.journalism.co.uk

CHAPTER 13

POLICE SERVICE

An introduction to the police service

The police service in the UK employs over 140,000 police officers including those employed by the British Transport Police. Graduate entrants are chosen for their potential to eventually lead others in a range of duties that may include counter-terrorism, Criminal Investigation Department (CID) and large-scale public events such as football matches and political demonstrations.

Police officers must be physically fit and have high personal integrity. You will undergo very stringent tests to see if you have the character to work in a demanding and often stressful context. Police officers, unlike the military, need to focus most of their attention on control and prevention. They need high levels of interpersonal skills to match the practical skills they learn in training. Police officers must not have a criminal record.

Police officer

What does a police officer do?

The role of the police is varied, but it essentially involves preventing and investigating crime. Other important aspects of the role include supporting the victims of crime, maintaining order, safety and security in the community, and responding to emergency calls and taking appropriate action when a call is logged. They are a high profile, uniformed presence on the streets and officers therefore need to have the confidence to work in such a public role. The job is both physically and emotionally demanding.

From time to time a police officer may be expected to attend court as part of a criminal trial. They may also work with community groups, schools and other organisations to provide advice and education. They work closely with the other emergency services (fire and ambulance) and with other agencies and professionals such as HM Revenue & Customs, immigration services, forensic scientists, social workers and the intelligence services.

Police officers patrol alone or with colleagues. Most patrol in a car or on a motorbike. The nature of the work means that police officers are often confronted with people who are distressed or aggressive. They sometimes have to work in difficult situations, such as the aftermath of a major incident such as an accident or bomb explosion. At other times they may need to make quick judgments to protect the safety of the public and other members of the force. A good level of physical fitness and mental alertness is vital.

Some officers are assigned to traffic control roles. Some forces have mounted police, river patrols and underwater search teams. British Transport Police officers patrol stations and trains. Most police officers are unarmed, but others do carry weapons when protecting sites deemed at high risk of terrorist attack, such as airports. Teams of specially trained armed police can be deployed quickly to attend firearms incidents anywhere in the UK.

The CID of a force investigates serious crimes; and some officers are part of squads that specialise in specific areas, such as drug crime, anti-terrorism initiatives, serious fraud and child protection.

In addition to regular recruitment drives, police forces want to attract high achievers for the High Potential Development (HPD) scheme – in particular men and women from under-represented groups. This scheme has been designed to support and develop future leaders of the police service, to improve their leadership and command skills and assist them to progress to senior positions. The police service benefits by receiving highly developed leaders to provide direction, take the service forward and respond to the challenges that the future holds. Graduates could reasonably be expected to join the HPD scheme. Promotion is based on merit, not length of service.

Sir Hugh Orde, former Chief Constable of the Police Service of Northern Ireland, and now president of the Association of Chief Police Officers, and the senior officer responsible for the HPD scheme said, 'The future of the police service depends on strong leadership. The HPD scheme plays a crucial role in identifying and developing our future leaders. We are looking for high achievers who we will support and develop in order to maximise their leadership and command skills in order to help them progress to senior positions.'

Two officers who have completed the scheme are Detective Chief Inspector Matt Ward and Sergeant Neal Craig. They comment that the scheme 'gives opportunities within the service to do and see things you would never do otherwise', and that a career as a police officer is exciting, demanding and rewarding. They comment that there 'are few other jobs open to graduates that provide the security, excitement, challenges and sheer job satisfaction of being a police officer'.

Key skills required

- Excellent communication and listening skills.
- Good physical fitness.
- An ability to relate well to different types of people, in sometimes dangerous and stressful situations.
- A good level of basic intelligence, alertness and a commitment to safeguarding the community and rule of law.
- There is a fair amount of paperwork, so an ability to keep good records and write well is important.
- IT literacy.
- An awareness of the need for tolerance and even-handedness when dealing with members of the public and integrity when dealing with confidential matters.

Entry routes

Entry to the graduate scheme obviously requires you to have a degree, but no subject is preferred over another. Non-graduates can also apply to join the police, but of course they cannot take the graduate entry route. Applicants must be over 17, and be a British, EU or Commonwealth citizen, or a foreign national with indefinite leave to remain in the UK.

All applicants undergo written tests, and a medical and fitness test will also form part of the assessment process. Police officers are also vetted to ensure that they do not represent a risk to the country. The police service actively tries to recruit from across the whole spectrum of society but applicants who have committed certain criminal offences will be ruled out, though people who have committed minor offences are not necessarily rejected. There are no height restrictions.

Training and development

All police officers go through a probationary period of two years. They learn through a combination of classroom study and practical experience.

All police forces use the national training system, the Initial Police Learning and Development Programme (IPLDP), which they adapt to local needs.

The training covers areas such as:

- criminal law
- managing crime scenes and suspects
- interviewing techniques
- police paperwork
- first aid
- equality and diversity.

Successful candidates in the HPD scheme can earn a postgraduate diploma in police leadership, and then a master's qualification.

Job prospects

There are more than 140,000 police officers working in the UK. There is not a single national force: the country is split into regions, each with its own discrete police force. In addition to the 43 regional forces, there are other forces such as the MOD Police, Transport Police and the Civil Nuclear Constabulary, which provide protection to the public and armed forces personnel. Recruitment occurs throughout the year, whenever vacancies arise.

Salary and other benefits

Police officers earn a similar basic wage wherever they are based in the UK, but allowances are made for officers who work in cities (particularly London), so their salaries will be higher than others.

A new graduate officer will earn £22,000 per annum, rising to around £25,000 in two to three years. As you are promoted (on merit) you can expect to earn up to £60,000 if you reach the grade of superintendent.

Further information

- British Transport Police, 25 Camden Road, London NW1 9LN. Tel: 0800 405040. Website: www.btprecruitment.com
- Civil Nuclear Constabulary, Culham Science Centre, Abingdon, Oxfordshire OX14 3DB. Tel: 01235 466666. Website: www.cnc.police. uk
- Ministry of Defence Police Recruiting Department, Building 66, MDP Wethersfield, Braintree, Essex CM7 4AZ. Website: modpoliceofficers. co.uk
- National Police Recruitment Team. Website: www.policecouldyou.co.uk
- *Real Life Guide: The Police Service*, Trotman Publishing

CHAPTER 14

SECURITY SERVICES

An introduction to the security services

I am grateful to the representative of the UK Security Services who collaborated with me to produce this profile. Its focus is on MI6 and Government Communications Headquarters (GCHQ). (Note: MI5 and MI6 look for very similar qualities in their applicants.)

The intelligence and security agencies (MI5, MI6 and GCHQ) work to protect our national security from internal threat (MI5) and external threat (MI6 and GCHQ). They work closely with the police, military and central government departments and most graduate entrants will have specific skills, such as a foreign language, to enable them to fulfil their role.

MI5 operates from its headquarters on the Thames in London. The Security Service Act 1989 defines MI5's role as 'the protection of national security and, in particular, its protection against threats from espionage, terrorism and sabotage, from the activities of agents of foreign powers and from actions intended to overthrow or undermine parliamentary democracy by political, industrial or violent means'.

To meet this role MI5 works with the police and others to prevent terrorism, prevent spies from other countries damaging our country and its reputation and stop weapons entering the country that might be used by terrorists.

They also work to reduce serious crime, such as drug- or people-trafficking and to protect important buildings (for example nuclear power stations, government buildings and transport networks) from those who might wish to destroy or illegally enter them.

MI6, also known as the Secret Intelligence Service (SIS), collects Britain's foreign intelligence. The service is based at Vauxhall Cross in London. SIS provides the government with a global covert capability to promote and defend the national security and economic wellbeing of the UK.

GCHQ, based in Cheltenham, Gloucestershire, works in partnership with MI5 and MI6 to protect the UK's national security interests. GCHQ has two important missions – signals intelligence (SIGINT) and information assurance (IA). SIGINT work provides vital information to support government policy-making and operations in the fields of national security, military operations, law enforcement and economic wellbeing. The intelligence GCHQ provides is at the heart of the struggle against terrorism and also contributes to the prevention and detection of serious crime. GCHQ also supplies crucial intelligence to the UK armed forces, wherever they are deployed in the world. IA is concerned with protecting government data – communications and information systems – from hackers and other threats.

Key skills required

Key skills for all three of the intelligence and security agencies include:

- common sense, confidence and good communication skills
- integrity
- the ability to work under pressure, at times in situations that are very dangerous, and to command respect under pressure
- the ability to work in a team and on your own
- being quick-witted and able to solve problems swiftly and without too much help
- clear leadership qualities.

MI5, MI6 and GCHQ have a very involved vetting process that checks the backgrounds of all applicants with great care.

MI5 and MI6

What do MI5 and MI6 do?

The clichéd view of MI5 and MI6 is that they are a mix of James Bond, John le Carré and the BBC series *Spooks*. In reality, their role has changed immensely in the last decade.

This profile focuses on MI6, which is the service that collects intelligence from outside the UK in order to protect security and economic wellbeing in the UK. All potential candidates will be required to undergo a positive vetting process that is expensive, exhaustive and designed to ensure that any applicant is capable of working in an environment that is both secretive and stressful. In essence, MI6 wants to make sure you do not have any skeletons in the cupboard that could be used against you in the future.

The role is split into three principal areas of interest to potential graduate entry candidates.

Operational officers

They perform a wide range of jobs including planning and carrying out intelligence operations overseas, recruiting and running agents and evaluating intelligence reports. These officers are as close to James Bond as one could reasonably get in the twenty-first century. Most of our operational officers have strong linguistic ability, initiative and an ability to influence and persuade people across cultural and linguistic boundaries. They need to be confident, have an interest in foreign affairs and have effective problem-solving skills. For obvious reasons they also need to have high levels of personal integrity and no significant criminal record.

Language specialists

These specialists spend their time translating documents and other intelligence material, including information found on internet sites and in media broadcasts. They are a vital part of the process that provides essential support for operating teams abroad. SIS employs graduates (and occasionally non-graduates) with ability in a variety of languages. At present they are particularly interested in people who can speak Arabic, Persian, Pashto, Russian, Chinese, French, German and Spanish. It is vital that the specialist is both fluent in one or more of these languages and also able to communicate clearly and accurately in written English. For this reason most language specialists are graduates who are fluent in both English and another language.

Science, IT and other professionals

The service also employs a number of scientists and IT professionals, recruited through a graduate recruitment scheme. Scientists are essentially involved in designing products that could be used operationally. IT specialists design and develop integrated cutting-edge IT support products and provide operational officers with world-class software solutions.

A range of other professionals work behind the scenes in an administrative capacity. These include specialists in human resource management, finance, procurement and project management.

Key skills required

- Applicants need to be men and women of integrity, honour and tact.
- They must be highly motivated and be able to work in an environment that is stressful and at times emotionally demanding.
- They need to have good organisation skills and be willing to work in a team of diverse professionals.
- They should have an active interest in foreign affairs and a desire to travel abroad, often to parts of the world that are challenging and potentially dangerous.

Entry requirements

Most applicants are graduates and they come from a wide variety of different academic disciplines. Clearly, an applicant who wishes to work in an operational role or as a translator, will benefit if they can speak one or more foreign languages fluently. However, that is not necessary if you wish to work in a department that does not require you to be posted abroad, for example in human resources (HR) or information technology (IT), where an appropriate alternative academic discipline such as human resource management, finance, computer science or any other mainstream academic discipline will suffice.

Training and development

MI5 and MI6 offer a comprehensive, role-specific in-house training programme.

Job prospects

MI5 and MI6 recruit all year round. They employ several thousand people who work both in London and overseas. The application process is somewhat protracted. All applications are processed online via their websites (www. mi6.gov.uk and www.mi5.gov.uk). All applicants must be British, aged over

21 and be willing to undergo a rigorous security clearance process. Successful applicants will undergo a medical and drugs test. Anyone who has taken a Class A drug in the last 12 months or a Class B or C drug in the last six months will fail the medical and will therefore not be able to take up the post. Applicants will be interviewed, undergo selection centre scrutiny and must not make their application known to anyone else.

Salary and other benefits

The salary will depend on the role you undertake. It is comparable with salaries in other Civil Service positions and a salary in excess of £30,000 is likely to be achievable fairly soon if you are competent. In addition, you receive access to private healthcare insurance, relocation expenses and other benefits such as gym membership, interest-free season ticket loans and childcare facilities.

Further information

- MI6,www.mi6.gov.uk
- MI5,www.mi5.gov.uk
- *Inside British Intelligence: 100 Years of MI5 and MI6*, Gordon Thomas

GCHQ

What does GCHQ do?

GCHQ – the Government Communications Headquarters – works in partnership with MI5 and MI6. The only security service based outside London (in Cheltenham, Gloucestershire), it plays a crucial role in countering threats to British people and interests. The remit of GCHQ is clearly defined and has two main elements:

- **signals intelligence (SIGINT)**: provides intelligence from communications and other signals in the interests of national security, the economic wellbeing of the UK, and the prevention and detection of serious crime

■ **information assurance (IA)**: works to protect and secure information on Government IT and communication systems from hackers and other threats. This work is carried out by the Communications–Electronics Security Group (CESG), a specialist organisation within GCHQ, and the National Technical Authority for Information Assurance.

GCHQ's customer base is diverse but primarily includes other government departments (such as the Ministry of Defence (MOD) and the Foreign and Commonwealth Office (FCO)).

What does a GCHQ employee do?

The jobs on offer at GCHQ are diverse, including anything from IT, internet and engineering roles, to intelligence analysts, linguists, finance experts, accountants and administrators. However, technology drives the work of GCHQ and all roles require individuals to have a certain level of familiarity with IT. The key job areas are as follows.

IT, internet and engineering

As the UK's technology-focused intelligence and security agency, GCHQ exploits all areas of technology to deliver its key functions of SIGINT and information assurance. The people it needs are engaged directly in various forms of IT such as software, hardware, telecommunications, research and development. Increasingly, the internet has become a focus for their work.

GCHQ recruits into the following technical disciplines.

■ **IT infrastructure engineering**: responsible for making sure the whole of GCHQ's IT infrastructure is fit for all its many purposes.
■ **IT service management**: making sure that GCHQ's IT systems are supplemented with robust processes in order to remain operational.
■ **Software engineering**: provides deployable engineering solutions in a well-managed and professional way.
■ **Telecommunications engineering**: finds innovative solutions to unique and often quite tricky challenges regarding the collection and processing of communications traffic and data.
■ **Information assurance**: provides advice and assistance on the security of communications and electronic data.

- **Internet operations**: responsible for analysing information from this continuously evolving source.
- **Systems engineering**: underpins the delivery of complex IT work programmes.
- **ICT research (applied research)**: researches emerging technologies and evaluates their potential; creates solutions to the risks they pose.
- **Project management**: responsible for the planning, implementation and delivery of GCHQ's projects.
- **Electrical and mechanical engineering**: responsible for a broad remit of services, covering system design, procurement and change management, as well as safety and radio frequency (RF) engineering.

Language and culture specialists (linguists)

GCHQ's linguists don't just understand foreign languages; they also understand their wider cultural application, in terms of historical, social, religious and regional differences. Work as a linguist in GCHQ involves being a frontline analyst, interpreting intelligence material (such as information found on websites and media broadcasts), putting the pieces together and using linguistic and cultural insights to shed light on the background to often headline stories. It provides an outlet for passionate language speakers who want to contribute to the UK's national security.

GCHQ requires skills in some rare and difficult languages, but also recruits individuals with more commonly learned languages (such as European languages) to retrain in other languages. Individuals who speak languages from the following regions are of particular interest to GCHQ:

- Eastern Europe
- the Middle East
- Asia
- Africa.

Intelligence analysts

At GCHQ information is collected from many sources and an intelligence analyst's role is to piece all the various bits of data together to provide advice and recommendations to GCHQ's customers. Analysts specialise in political and military topics appropriate to their area of work, and are encouraged to diversify by moving to different analytical posts. This means they gain a broad understanding of the whole range of intelligence topics, although they often specialise in one area. Individuals for these types of roles need to be lateral thinkers, so an agile and enquiring mind is essential, as is a flexible nature (due to the demands of the work). These roles are often customer-facing, so individuals are responsible for representing GCHQ in the public domain. More and more analytical roles are becoming IT orientated, so individuals with experience in this area are also desirable.

Mathematicians

GCHQ is one of the few places outside academia where individuals can practise advanced mathematical research, and pit their wits against other mathematicians. The teams include some of the nation's top mathematical minds working on some of the world's most challenging cryptographic problems. They are supported by cutting-edge IT and training. GCHQ is an ideal workplace for the able mathematician with a good degree in maths or a related discipline, not to mention a passion for problem solving.

Corporate support

Like all major organisations, GCHQ is a self-contained business unit. In order to deliver its core operational work, the organisation recruits into the following support areas:

- accountancy and finance
- administration
- audit
- contracts management
- commercial managers
- purchasing and procurement
- vetting officers.

Key skills required

In addition to any necessary qualifications or experience (as specified for each vacancy), GCHQ looks for the following:

- integrity and a desire to work in the intelligence field
- an ability to work as part of a team
- leadership potential

- good organisational skills and the ability to drive things forward
- flexibility to deal with a fast-paced and emotionally demanding work environment
- an analytical nature and good decision-making ability
- an understanding of what constitutes good customer service
- excellent communications skills
- a willingness to share knowledge
- proficiency with IT.

For any role at GCHQ, individuals will be required to provide evidence of their accomplishments and achievements in the areas above.

Job prospects

Many of the roles at GCHQ demand specific skills and knowledge, and will only be open to graduates with relevant degrees. However, there are opportunities for non-graduates and individuals with relevant experience. Due to the nature of GCHQ's work it is not possible for individuals to undertake work experience, but the organisation does offer some sponsorship/placement opportunities for undergraduates studying technical degrees. Occasionally GCHQ also offers an apprenticeship scheme to recruit trainee electronics and electrical engineers; the entry criterion for this scheme is five GCSEs (grades A–C) or equivalent, which must include English language, mathematics and a science subject.

Regardless of role, everyone is encouraged to diversify in their career and move from post to post approximately every three years. This means the work remains interesting and challenging, and also gives individuals the opportunities to develop new skills. In all areas, individuals receive the necessary support and structured training to enable them to be effective on the job.

GCHQ recruits all year round and employs several thousand people who work predominantly in Cheltenham, although there are also station sites in Bude (Cornwall) and Scarborough (North Yorkshire). The application process is very thorough, due to the sensitive nature of the work. Applications are initially processed online via the GCHQ careers website (www.gchq-careers. co.uk). Individuals will then be subject to various assessment methods (such as interviews, written tests, group exercises and selection days) to determine their suitability for employment. All applicants must (as a minimum) be

British citizens, over the age of 18, and be willing to undergo a rigorous security clearance process. Successful applicants will undergo medical scrutiny and a drugs test, and must also limit whom they tell about their application. All employees sign the Official Secrets Act on their first day.

Salary and other benefits

The salary will depend on the role. Support level salaries are in the region of £16,000–19,000, while graduate starting salaries are around £25,000. Individuals with certain 'hard to recruit' skills (for example, rare language speakers) may receive a bonus payment. All employees are members of the Civil Service pension scheme and have access to a range of other benefits, including:

- generous holiday allowances
- maternity and paternity leave
- childcare facilities
- flexible working patterns
- employee assistance service
- union representation.

Further information

- *GCHQ Careers* www.gchq-careers.co.uk

CASE STUDY: RIK, INTELLIGENCE ANALYST

Why did you decide to join GCHQ?

I came across GCHQ during my last year of A levels. I'd decided I didn't want to go to university and had started looking for training opportunities or for that 'first' job. I'd never considered a job in intelligence but I found a copy of GCHQ's latest recruitment brochure in my careers library and was intrigued by what they did. I presumed anyone working in an intelligence agency would have to have a degree, so I was really pleased to discover there were opportunities for me.

What's your career progression been like?

I've had quite a varied career so far! I started in FLITS – First Line IT Support – this entailed working in a helpdesk environment, ensuring GCHQ personnel could make the best use of IT systems. From that I naturally progressed to managing aspects of the helpdesk; in particular I was responsible for looking after the actual helpdesk employees – making sure they had the necessary training, for example. After that I changed direction completely, and took up the position I currently occupy of intelligence analyst. This is a really challenging role, and I've had to learn lots of new skills, but I love being part of GCHQ's main operational work!

What are the best bits?

For me there are two aspects. First, I love the thrill of working on real stuff that applies to the here and now; there's nothing more rewarding than watching the news, seeing a story break, and knowing I contributed to that in some way. Second, the training and support I've received. Initially, I was a bit concerned about becoming an intelligence analyst, as the normal entry requirement is a degree. I thought I might feel out of my depth, but I haven't found this at all, and I know I am valued for what I do regardless of my academic background.

Is there anything you'd change?

Sometimes it is frustrating not being able to tell everyone exactly what it is I do, but to be honest you soon get used to it. Other than that the only thing I can really think of is the way in which we are often perceived to be 'spies', in the same vein as James Bond. There is frequently misunderstanding around what GCHQ does, and many people make the mistake of thinking we are MI5 and MI6. All three agencies have their own identity and are unique in what they do; it just happens to be that we come together with one central mission – to safeguard UK interests.

CASE STUDY: CHRISTINE, INFORMATION ASSURANCE CONSULTANT

What is a typical day at GCHQ like?

Here comes the first cliché – there really isn't a typical day – especially for me. I work a four-day compressed working week. That means that the first day back involves a lot of catching up! I normally wake myself up with a nice cup of coffee while I catch up with my manager about the week ahead. This morning, I spent a few hours redrafting a document I had submitted that needed to be with a customer by midday. No sooner had I hit the 'send' button than I overheard a conversation. I couldn't help but join in and add my thoughts. We have lots of informal chats like that. It's great for knowledge sharing. Tomorrow I'm doing a presentation to a government department; the day after I am working on a document detailing a new secure PDA. Variety isn't the word!

What are the best bits?

I just love new technology. At the moment I'm doing a lot of work on mobile security. The idea is to allow government customers to use classified data while on the move. The training is intense and fascinating. I've had classroom lessons, but I also went overseas to a hackers' conference last year. It's all about being one step ahead.

Tell us more about the environment.

Well, the building is pretty big, but I work in a relatively normal open plan office. I say 'relatively' – the subjects we talk about are often pretty technical, but that's what excites me. The local area's also got loads to offer. There's a great mix of town and country, so pretty much whatever you're into you can still enjoy. Whether that's hiking boots or kitten heels, real ale or kir royale.

CHAPTER 15

TEACHING

An introduction to teaching

A career in teaching covers a whole range of different options, from nursery education through to higher education. This chapter focuses primarily on primary and secondary roles.

All of us have experience of teaching as a profession, if only from the perspective of a pupil. This perspective can colour our judgment and create a false image of the profession. What this profile intends to do is to create an impression that is fair and honest, bringing the profession into the twenty-first century and dispelling those myths that persist.

Teaching is an important and increasingly popular choice of career for all kinds of people. Whatever your circumstances – if you're still at school, about to graduate, or looking for a change of direction – there are more ways to enter the profession than ever before.

The first issue to consider is what age group you want to teach. The majority of children in the UK start formal education in a playgroup or nursery. While this is a vital part of the education system, the majority of graduates joining the profession choose to be either infant/primary specialists or secondary specialists. Children start infant education at the age of 5, when they join the Foundation Year programme. Most finish primary education in Year 6 at the age of 11. At this point most, but not all, children enter the secondary sector and stay until Year 11 when they complete their GCSE qualifications. An increasing number stay on at 16 and start A level or equivalent qualifications in the sixth form (Years 12/13) before leaving school for good.

At this point many people start work, but those who remain in full-time education will encounter the next type of teaching professional, the higher or further education specialist. University education brings with it new challenges as a teacher (or lecturer) as it is a role that is combined with research into whichever field of education you, the teacher, wish to pursue. Many undergraduates are taught by post-MA students who are doing PhDs as well as full-time postdoctoral lecturers and professors. In the further education world, teachers spend more time teaching than doing research and tend to work in adult education colleges rather than universities. Both roles are important, but they are very different.

One organisation that is promoting teaching to a new generation of young graduates and trying to break down the barriers that exist in the world of education is Teach First. This is an independent charity launched in 2002 to bring excellent teachers into challenged secondary schools across the UK. Further details of this scheme can be found under 'Entry routes' below.

Schoolteacher – primary and secondary

What does a schoolteacher do?

A schoolteacher is a professional who is trained to educate children in a variety of different environments. Formal education starts at the age of 5 in the Foundation Year of an infant school. When a child reaches the age of 7 they move on to the junior stage. The infant and junior stages constitute Primary education and many children will go to a primary school between the ages of 5 and 11 rather than separate infant and junior schools. At 11 they go to a secondary school, where most stay until they are 16. A significant number stay on into the sixth form; others go to work or stay in further education in a college or via an Apprenticeship. In some areas education is structured differently and children may go to a middle school between the ages of 8 and 13. Some independent (private) schools have a prep school (Years 0–9) and a senior school (Years 9–12).

All the famous and successful entrepreneurs in the UK have one thing in common: they had teachers. Teachers also play an essential part in helping children and young people to acquire the knowledge and social, cultural and practical skills they will need throughout their lives in order to become rounded adult members of society. The work involves building relationships with pupils that encourage them to learn and fulfil their potential.

Teachers spend most of their time teaching, but they have a range of other duties, which may include:

- preparing material to use in the classroom
- marking

- keeping records
- managing behaviour inside and outside the classroom
- coaching sports teams, directing plays or conducting musical ensembles
- meeting with parents to discuss a child's progress
- liaising with other professionals such as social workers, welfare officers and at times the police.

Most teaching professionals specialise in teaching at either an infant/primary or a secondary school.

In the research that I carried out I spoke to teachers in the primary, secondary and higher education sectors. The advice in this chapter is therefore based not only on my experience as a teacher but also on the experience of other full-time professionals. One key message all have given is the need to get as much experience in school as you can before choosing to embark on your career. Most schools are more than happy to accommodate people who want to observe classes or work as unpaid teacher assistants. In some instances this may require you to undertake a police or Criminal Records Bureau (CRB) check, but the pay-off is well worth it.

Key skills required

- Excellent communication skills.
- A passion for your subject and the desire to encourage others to enjoy the subject too.
- Confidence when talking to an audience.
- Patience, enthusiasm and stamina.
- A good sense of humour.
- The ability to work on your own as well as in a team.
- A willingness to deal with sometimes aggressive or unacceptable behaviour (this is far less likely in a higher education context).
- The ability to work to tight deadlines.
- The academic ability to reach the standards of the training course.

A university lecturer also needs to be willing to undertake original academic research to advance their specialised subject and enhance the reputation of the university that they represent.

Entry routes

The vast majority of teachers are graduates who have also taken a one-year postgraduate qualification that allows them to teach. This is called a PGCE (Postgraduate Certificate in Education) and is taken, after you graduate, at a university that offers teacher training. Teachers are employed by the state or by a private educational institution. Most work in state schools: others are employed by the armed forces, city academies, young offenders' units, prisons or further education colleges.

There are around 470,000 teachers working in the education sector and it remains a popular career choice. There is a particular demand for certain specialist teachers in under-resourced subjects – these include mathematics, chemistry, physics, religious education, ICT and design and technology.

Teachers must have GCSEs (A*–C) in English and maths and, in the case of primary teaching, a science subject. The new Diploma in Society, Health and Development, available in many schools and colleges, may be relevant for this work.

The main entry routes are:

- Bachelor of Education (BEd) degree taking three or four years to complete on a full-time basis, or four to six years part time. Applicants normally require a minimum of five GCSEs (A*–C) and two A levels or equivalent, but you should check with individual institutions as entry requirements can vary
- BA/BSc degree with QTS (Qualified Teacher Status) with the same entry requirements as a BEd
- Postgraduate Certificate in Education (PGCE), an intensive teacher training course completed in one year full time or two years part time. A degree that is relevant to the PGCE you are studying for is normally required. This is by far and away the most common route into teaching.

These courses are all undertaken at a university or college and are available throughout the UK. Each of these routes includes placements, in which trainees undertake supervised teaching practice in two different schools.

Two other alternatives open to some graduates are:

- Teach First – a programme during which graduates spend two years teaching in a challenging school or referral unit, gaining both QTS and commercial skills. Teach First is aimed mainly at secondary-level teaching. Entry requirements are at least a 2:1 degree: either the degree or an A level (at grade A or B) must involve a National Curriculum subject. Candidates must demonstrate leadership qualities and other personal attributes.

■ Graduate Teacher Programme (GTP) – allows graduates to train while working and earning as unqualified teachers. GTP usually takes a year.

Primary teacher

What do primary teachers do?

Primary teachers teach pupils aged from five to 11 and have responsibility for one class. They cover all subjects of the National Curriculum (NC) at Key Stage 1 or 2. The core subjects are English, maths and science, which are taught alongside a range of other subjects including design and technology (DT), information and communication technology (ICT), history, geography, languages, art and design, music and physical education (PE). Some primary teachers are specialists who travel between a group of schools teaching subjects such as PE, music or art.

The main challenge facing the primary teacher is the fact that, unlike their counterparts in the secondary and HE sector, they teach a whole class for the majority of the day. While there are specialist primary teachers with particular interests in science, art or maths, the bulk of the teaching is delivered by one key individual. It is therefore vital that these teachers deliver the National Curriculum well to every child and that the lessons cater for both the able and less able. Managing children with special educational needs is common and this is another real challenge, in terms of both classroom management and lesson preparation.

It is a popular misconception that primary teaching (and all teaching for that matter) is an easy nine-to-three job. The reality is that a lot of hard work takes place outside these times and good teachers will inevitably find themselves taking work home with them or preparing lesson plans at the weekend.

Secondary teacher

What do secondary teachers do?

Secondary school teachers work with pupils aged between 11 and 19. They usually specialise in teaching one or two NC subjects at Key Stages 3 and 4. Some may also teach vocational subjects. Key Stage 3 subjects include English, maths, science, design and technology, ICT, history, geography, languages, art and design, music, citizenship and PE. A large part of a teacher's job focuses on preparing pupils for external examinations such as GCSE and A levels.

Most teachers work a nine-to-five day, although preparation work can mean that you work longer hours and into the weekends. Holidays are good and this is a major perk of the job. Teachers must attend parents' evenings and are encouraged to participate in activities outside school hours. They may sometimes accompany pupils on trips locally or abroad. Some teachers may also have to attend meetings outside school hours.

A particular challenge for the secondary teacher is classroom management. Teenagers are well known for their behaviour swings, so a firm control of the class is vital. All my years' experience of teaching suggests that you need to have the character to deal with poor behaviour quickly and firmly. Children actually quite like firm and clear boundaries (whatever they may say to the contrary!) and teachers who have good control of classes and can at times be strict are actually well liked.

Salary

(Salaries quoted apply to state-maintained schools.) A newly qualified teacher starts on £21,000 a year (£25,000 in inner London). An experienced unpromoted teacher earns £30,148 a year (£34,768 in inner London). Head teachers may earn from £40,494 to £100,424, depending on the size of the school (up to £107,192 in inner London).

University (HE) lecturer

What does a university lecturer do?

University lecturers are sometimes called higher education (HE) lecturers. Their role is to deliver courses leading to Higher National Awards, degrees and postgraduate qualifications such as master's degrees and PGCEs. They tend to teach a subject in which they have a high level of qualification. Not all lecturers have PhDs, but most have postgraduate degrees such as an MA or MSc. These are taken after completing your first degree and mark you out as an expert in your field.

The job is varied and will involve many other roles in addition to teaching. All HE lecturers will undertake some form of personal research in their chosen area of expertise, devise schemes of work, mark scripts and supervise those doing master's or PhD courses. They work in higher education establishments, such as universities, and do not come into contact with children on a day-to-day basis. The skills required are broadly similar to those of the classroom teacher in a school. However, you will also need a high standard of research skills and a passion for the subject that enables you to push against the boundaries of what is currently known or agreed.

Most HE lecturers work in one of the 190 HE institutions in the UK. Others work for specialist colleges such as the College of Law. There are 13,000 HE lecturers working in the UK. Around 60% are on full-time contracts; the others are employed on an annual contract or part-time basis.

A formal postgraduate teaching qualification was recently introduced for all HE lecturers. This course is now compulsory for all entrants to the profession and is taken during your first year in post. It is accredited by the Higher Education Academy and involves day release and evening work.

Further information

- *Teaching Uncovered*, Trotman Publishing
- *Working in Schools and Colleges*, VT Lifeskills
- *Working in English*, VT Lifeskills

CHAPTER 16

VETERINARY SCIENCE

An introduction to veterinary science

The vetinary profession is a competitive but highly rewarding sector that offers anyone with a love of animals the opportunity to work in an environment that will enable them to be directly involved in their care and protection. It is vital that you are able to meet the difficult academic demands of entry to the profession and that you show in any application you make that you have both experience of working with animals and an awareness of the demands of the profession in a changing world.

Veterinarians provide healthcare for all animals, including farm livestock (sheep, cows and poultry being the most common), pets (birds, cats, dogs, etc), and zoo, sporting and laboratory animals. It is a legal requirement that all establishments that use animals for research, such as drug companies, employ both animal technicians (who are trained to handle animals) and qualified vets to ensure that the animals are healthy and cared for appropriately.

Most working vets perform clinical work in private practices. Of these, most work with small animals, treating injuries and illness and administering inoculations and health checks. This is the most common way in which the general public come into contact with the profession. A good vet must have the personal qualities to deal with a variety of different clients, some of whom will be anxious and demanding.

A small number of private practice vets work exclusively with large animals, in particular horses and cows. They usually drive to stables or farms to provide services for individual animals or herds. This involves treating conditions or injuries, plus preventive care to maintain herd health, such as inoculation. They also consult with owners on animal management. Most of these vets are employed in private practice too, but will be based in rural areas.

Some vets also work in public health and research at universities. A small number are employed by the government, for instance in the Department for the Environment, Food and Rural Affairs (DEFRA). Others work for major charities whose primary focus is animal welfare. The largest of these employers in the UK is the RSPCA.

The training is long and hard but the job is ultimately highly rewarding, both financially and personally.

A veterinary surgeon

What does a veterinary surgeon do?

Making the decision to become a veterinary surgeon will set you on a course for one of the most varied and exciting careers available. The veterinary profession offers many diverse and stimulating career opportunities, as well as the privilege of working with animals.

A vet is trained in a wide range of animal care techniques, including the prescription of drugs, surgery, vaccination programmes, assisting with births, setting fractures and using X-ray equipment. Most vets work in small-animal practices and their day-to-day duties include:

- diagnosing animal health problems
- vaccinating against diseases, such as influenza, rabies and distemper
- medicating animals suffering from infections or illnesses
- treating and dressing wounds
- setting fractures
- performing surgery
- advising owners about animal care
- inserting identification microchips
- performing a euthanisia on animals that are beyond treatment
- providing paperwork for animals travelling abroad
- dealing with out of hours emergencies.

Vets may also be employed in industry, the two most common areas being drug development and animal feed production.

The hours vets work are varied but can be long and unsociable at times. In group practices, vets often take turns being on call for evening, night or weekend work. Vets in large-animal practices spend much of their time driving between their practice and local farms or riding stables. In addition, large-animal vets work almost entirely in the open air, in all weathers and in sometimes smelly conditions! Contact with animals that are frightened or in pain is common and vets are not immune from personal injury. The work can also be physically hard and tiring.

Key skills required

The University of Nottingham has a new but respected veterinary school, which looks for the following attributes in their applicants. Any other veterinary school will look for the same skills: they reflect the abilities you will need to work as a vet after you have graduated.

- Academically you should be able to show good overall achievement at GCSE and A level, including high grades in science subjects.
- As a vet you will need good communication skills - listening, writing and speaking - and good hand-eye co-ordination, dexterity and precision of motor skills.
- All vet schools will expect you to have gained some animal-focused work experience, preferably in a range of animal-related areas such as at a veterinary practice, working with horses or on a farm, at a zoo or wildlife park, in research or laboratory settings or even spending time at an abattoir.
- You are expected to have an understanding of the positive and negative aspects of a veterinary career and have an awareness of current important issues and developments in veterinary medicine and science.
- You must have a number of personal attitudes and attributes that are needed to be successful both on the course and in a veterinary career. These include a caring ethos (compassion, tolerance, patience, empathy) and a sense of social responsibility.
- You should be able to cope with change and uncertainty and to overcome challenges while understanding your own limitations.
- You need self-motivation, self-confidence, self-reliance and initiative.
- You should be able to show that you have the ability to work independently and as part of a team, to integrate, co-operate and be flexible.
- Good personal organisational skills and time management skills are a must.

Entry routes

All vets are required to take a professional qualification at a licensed veterinary school. Studying veterinary medicine and science at university will allow you to gain the professionally recognised qualification that will allow you to practise as a veterinary surgeon.

Only seven institutions offer veterinary medicine in the UK – Bristol, Cambridge, Edinburgh, Glasgow, Liverpool, London (Royal Veterinary College) and Nottingham. Competition is high, but it is a myth that you need to be exceptionally academic. However, you should be able to show good overall achievement at GCSE level, including high grades in science subjects. At A2 level, most vet schools will expect students to have studied biology and chemistry, and to have achieved high grades in these subjects. There are now other entry routes into vet school, including the preliminary year at Nottingham (which accepts students with high grades in non-science or vocational subjects).

There are also widening participation courses specifically aimed at learners from under-represented groups, such as the Gateway course run at RVC and the Veterinary Science Certificate course at Lincoln (for progression to Nottingham) – these courses generally look for grades CCC at A2 level. The Gateway course is specific to the RVC but other schools run outreach programmes and they are all very keen to recruit young people from across the social spectrum. If you are academically able, have a passion for animals and animal welfare and are willing to work hard they are keen for you to apply. Interestingly, they are very keen for more male applicants as it is a profession that in recent years has been very female-oriented in its applicant profile.

Candidates also need to show they have gained a range of practical experience of working with animals. This might include visiting a laboratory or voluntary work at stables, farms or kennels, or shadowing a vet in practice.

Salary

A recent graduate's salary will depend largely on the practice that they join. However, as a rule of thumb a new vet could expect to earn in the region of £30,000. This can rise to over £100,000 if you end up leading a large practice.

Job prospects

There are more than 20,000 veterinary surgeons in the UK. Most work in private practice. There are other opportunities with a wide range of different employers including zoos, animal charities, government agencies such as DEFRA and the Royal Army Veterinary Corps.

Further information

- Association of Veterinary Students. Website: www.avs-uk.org.uk
- Government Veterinary Surgeons, c/o Department for Environment, Food and Rural Affairs, Area 5D, Nobel House, 17 Smith Square, London SW1P 3JR. Website: www.defra.gov.uk/gvs
- PDSA (People's Dispensary for Sick Animals), Whitechapel Way, Priorslee, Telford, Shropshire TF2 9PQ. Tel: 01952 290999. Website: www.pdsa.org.uk
- Royal College of Veterinary Surgeons (RCVS), Belgravia House, 62-64 Horseferry Road, London SW1P 2AF. Tel: 020 7222 2001. Websites: www.rcvs.org.uk and www.walksoflife.org.uk
- RSPCA (Royal Society for the Prevention of Cruelty to Animals), Wilberforce Way, Southwater, Horsham, West Sussex RH13 9RS. Tel: 0300 1234 555. Website: www.rspca.org.uk
- *Getting into Veterinary School*, Trotman Publishing
- *Training to be a Veterinary Surgeon*, RCVS